BACK IN THE BIGS

BY RANDY TURNER

Winnipeg Free Press

BACK IN THE BIGS

ISBN 978-0-9682575-6-2

Printed in Canada

LIBRARY AND ARCHIVES CANADA CATALOGUING IN PUBLICATION

Turner, Randy, 1961-
Back in the bigs / by Randy Turner.

ISBN 978-0-9682575-6-2

1. Winnipeg Jets (Hockey team). 2. National Hockey League. 3. Hockey--Manitoba--Winnipeg--History. I. Title.

GV848.W56T87 2011 796.962'6409712743 C2011-905634-8

First printing

Written by: Randy Turner
Project editor: Julie Carl
Book editor: Buzz Currie
Art director / production: Gordon Preece
Photo editor: Mike Aporius
Research: Ken Gigliotti, Alexandra Paul, Ed Tait
Proofreaders: Jason Bell, Ron Campbell, Andrew Maxwell and Teghan Beaudette

The Winnipeg Free Press extends its thanks to the librarians and archivists who went out of their way to track down historical photographs for this book.
The Winnipeg Tribune photographs from the city's period with the World Hockey Association are stored at the Elizabeth Dafoe Library at the University of Manitoba.
Each photo credited to the Winnipeg Tribune is part of a collection at the University of Manitoba Archives and Special Collections.

COVER PHOTO / Bobby Hull skates in a game against the Quebec Nordiques of the WHA on March 3, 1976. — Jon Thordarson Winnipeg Tribune, U of M Archives

Distributed by Penguin Group (Canada) (A Division of Pearson Canada, Inc.) 90 Eglinton Ave. East, Suite 700 Toronto, ON M4P 2Y3

 All Winnipeg Jets logos and marks used in this book are with permission from the Winnipeg Jets Hockey Club.

THE raucous crowd fell silent as Winnipeg businessman Mark Chipman began to speak at the National Hockey League draft in St. Paul June 24, 2011. I watched him live, along with thousands of Winnipeg hockey fans, proud that he was there, so proud that we were back in the NHL — but wondering just how he would address our "no-name" status.

And then the magic words:

"General manager Kevin Cheveldayoff will be making this pick... on behalf of The Winnipeg Jets."

Fans erupted in applause in Minnesota, in Winnipeg, in the Free Press newsroom. And there were tears in my eyes — me, who hadn't seen an NHL game since the '90s with my dad in the old arena.

The Jets were back.

Obviously, it was about more than hockey. It was about who we are.

The NHL franchise was always a point of pride in Winnipeg, once the third-largest city in Canada, then fourth, now clinging to eighth place. The Jets put Winnipeg on the map; everybody from Finland to Philadelphia knew Bobby Hull and Teemu Selanne.

The struggle to keep the team in its final years was heartbreaking.

How many times can you hear you're too small and too poor to ever support a big-league team? When they packed up and left, we lost more than an NHL team, we lost faith in our future.

"The Guess Who suck, the Jets were lousy anyway," John K. Samson of The Weakerthans sang in 2003.

It was the perfect reflection of Winnipeg's ever-present public persona... self-deprecating, self-loathing.

You'll never hear Prairie folk boast about being "world class." It's too easy to set yourself up for those oh-so-funny Winterpeg jokes. We wear our armour for a reason.

But these days, underneath that quintessential Prairie schtick, there runs a fierce and immutable pride.

The Jets have returned. And our faith has, too.

It's a helluva story.

Thanks to author and Free Press sportswriter Randy Turner for telling it so well.

Margo Goodhand
Editor
Winnipeg Free Press

CHAPTER 1 **A NEW BEGINNING** / 1

CHAPTER 2 **THE GOLDEN JET** / 21

CHAPTER 3 **THE JETS TAKE OFF** / 43

CHAPTER 4 **A SWEDISH RHAPSODY** / 55

CHAPTER 5 **FERGUSON'S JETS** / 79

CHAPTER 6 **FINNISH FLASH** / 103

CHAPTER 7 **THE JETS CRASH** / 129

CHAPTER 8 **ZINGER AND KITTY** / 155

CHAPTER 9 **CHIPMAN IN CHARGE** / 177

CHAPTER 10 **BACK IN THE BIGS** / 203

BACK IN
THE
BIGS

Fans turn out to Portage and Main bright and early the morning of May 31, 2011 when it was announced the NHL was coming back to Winnipeg. Antony Maluzynsky (second from left) and Cody Petrash (third from left) were the first to arrive at the iconic street corner.

KEN GIGLIOTTI WINNIPEG FREE PRESS

CHAPTER ONE:

A New Beginning

IT'S dusk at the corner of Portage and Main on the day the National Hockey League finds its way back to Winnipeg, and a 21-year-old bricklayer is cradling the hopes and dreams of a generation of Manitoba hockey fans, as well as a half-empty two-four of Great Western.

The trademark wind that defines the historic intersection is howling, strong enough to push Sidney Crosby off his skates if he'd been lucky enough to be there. Rain is spitting sideways. It's unseasonably cold and miserable as the clock ticks down on the third period of May.

But Brad Gebhardt couldn't care less. The smile plastered on his face is a reflection of a province gripped in NHL rapture. Or better yet, resurrection.

'I don't think Winnipeg ever gave up on getting an NHL team back'

— Brad Gebhardt

Gebhardt was just six years old when the Winnipeg Jets left town. He claims to have attended the last game. If every Manitoban who insisted they were there the night the Jets lost 4-1 to the Detroit Red Wings on April 28, 1996 — an evening far more miserable, but for many different reasons — the old barn must have seated a few hundred thousand instead of the sellout crowd of 15,567. But maybe Brad Gebhardt was in that crowd.

No matter. Gebhardt is a young man now, revelling with a dozen or so 20-somethings, waving frantically at passing cars amid chants of "Go Jets Go!" They were the hardy remnants of the few thousand Winnipeggers who earlier had flocked like homing pigeons to the very spot where Bobby Hull became professional hockey's first millionaire some 40 years before.

Metaphorically, the Jets were born at Portage and Main. They died there, too.

And whether you were six or 60, it stung all the same.

"You feel lost," Gebhardt said. "It's heartbreaking. You don't know who to cheer for. I was at the last Jets game and I've been wanting them back ever since. You're never going to give up. I don't think Winnipeg ever gave up on getting an NHL team back."

But the team did come back. It became official earlier that same day, May 31, 2011, when a car dealer-turned-NHL owner named Mark Chipman stepped up to a podium in the bowels of the MTS Centre and proclaimed, "I'm excited beyond words to announce our purchase of the Atlanta Thrashers." And it was young Winnipeggers who rejoiced in the streets, took up sticks for a spontaneous street hockey game at Portage and Main or bathed themselves in cheap champagne at The Forks. Most of them would have been in grade school and some in nursery school when the Jets bid Winnipeg the long, tearful goodbye and vanished into the Arizona desert.

The vast majority would never have even seen Dale Hawerchuk play, much less known to call him "Ducky." For them, Hull, the Golden Jet, would be more myth than real and the World Hockey Association an ancient, bygone era told in stories passed down by their fathers. Or grandfathers.

'I'm excited beyond words to announce our purchase of the Atlanta Thrashers'

— Mark Chipman

DAVID LIPNOWSKI THE CANADIAN PRESS ARCHIVES

CHIPMAN

A bird's-eye view of Portage and Main

KEN GIGLIOTTI WINNIPEG FREE PRESS

Kristian Rents at the celebrations at Portage and Main after Winnipeggers learned the NHL was coming back to the city.

Yet there was Gebhardt, arm in arm with his JFF (Jets friend forever) Andrew Lima, all of 26. Said Gebhardt of Lima: "I've known this kid for two years and every day he wears something with a Jets logo on it. He keeps the Jets with him every day."

It's true. Lima, a bicycle technician at a sporting goods store, has a collection that includes two Jets jerseys, five hats and four shirts, along with dozens of other knick-knacks.

Remember: This is merchandise for a team that vanished 15 years ago, when Lima was entering the fifth grade. How can you explain such a phenomenon?

For Lima, the answer is no mystery at all.

"It's hard to understand why your team had to leave at that young age, when you're so impressionable," he said. "It's like every other city had a hockey team and you can't understand why your team had to move so far away. Now you can't watch the heroes you grew up watching play.

"It's surreal. It still feels like a dream that we got the team back. It hasn't fully sunk in."

Fans crowd around
the big-screen
closed-circuit TV a
Canwest Place Ma
31, 2011 to watch th
announcement tha
the NHL was comin
back to town

Twelve-year-old
Matt Guenther minds
the net in a massive
game of pickup hockey
at Portage and Main

Watching the big screen at The Forks.

FINALLY THE NATIONAL HOCKEY LEAGUE HAS COME BACK TO WINNIPEG! LONG TIME COMING

Hooting and hollering at Portage and Main as the announcement is made.

Willow Parke (left) and Kaylee Allan scream for joy as they celebrate at The Forks.

A fan raises an inflatable Stanley Cup over his head in victory.

RUTH BONNEVILLE WINNIPEG FREE PRESS

Scampering across the barriers at Portage and Main.

KEN GIGLIOTTI WINNIPEG FREE PRESS

The night celebration at Portage and Main May 31, 2011.

'The trademark wind that defines the historic intersection is howling, strong enough to push Sidney Crosby off his skates if he'd been lucky enough to be there. Rain is spitting sideways. It's unseasonably cold and miserable as the clock ticks down on the third period of May'

Former Winnipeg Jet Thomas Steen signs autographs at The Forks as hundreds of fans gather to celebrate the return of the NHL.

It was as though the Dodgers found their way back to Brooklyn.

At The Forks, on the banks of the Red River, they came on that day of rebirth like salmon swimming upstream, by the thousands. It was a revolving door of human mayhem. They came wearing their Jets jerseys. They came in hockey equipment. They came painted blue.

One man, a 37-year-old accountant named Mike Bailey, arrived dressed up as Santa on a silver Harley-Davidson. He posed for pictures and wished one and all a "Merry Jetsmas."

It was a social on steroids. They sang *O Canada*. They chanted "We Want Teemu." On the street corner, a guy was selling T-shirts

with a picture of the NHL commissioner flashing a maniacal smile and in bold letters, "Gary Bettman Sucks." Someone asked, "Is that picture real?" The hawker shrugged and said, "We brightened his teeth."

Everyone and his dog was there. Literally. Tom Hildahl walked by with his girlfriend Miriam Waldman and his dog, Mica, who was clad in a Jets jersey. "It's kid-sized," Hildahl grinned. And the mutt seemed to be smiling, too.

The euphoria spanned generations. Dale Wohlgemuth was holding his two-year-old grandson, Judah, who was sporting a Jets jersey once worn by his father, Matt, now 28. They were soaking up the atmosphere at The Forks while Van Halen's *Jump* — the theme song that was the background noise at the arena during the '80s and '90s — blared over the loudspeakers.

"It was a roller-coaster and sometimes it wasn't much fun," Wohlgemuth said. "We had to go through this withdrawal. But it was pretty gratifying to sit with Matt and Judah this morning and watch that press conference.

"We didn't think they were going to come back. We thought we were done. We tried to cheer for the Coyotes, but that didn't work. We went to Toronto for a game, but it wasn't the same. It was very hard. Very hard. I mean, it was our team. I followed them since 1972. I used to listen to them on a little transistor radio.

"We lost them once. But they're coming back. And I'd say that's a feel-good story if there ever was one."

Lima was right. It was surreal. After all, it was during the dark days of 1995 and 1996 — a heart-wrenching period when all the desperate efforts to save the Jets had been tried and failed — that both The Forks and Portage and Main became beachheads for tens of thousands of civilian troops rallying to the cause. Remember those stories of kids who emptied their piggy banks?

One of them was Will Stangeland, then age seven, whose father told him, "Do you want your allowance or do you want to save the Jets?"

Young Willie chose the latter.

On the day the NHL came back, a 23-year-old Stangeland was found at The Forks on a night so frigid he could see his breath. Undaunted, he was wearing a Bauer helmet and hockey pants — and nothing else. His bare chest and legs were painted blue.

"It's exciting and overwhelming," he said, shivering against the cold. "I can't wait. But until they drop the puck, I won't believe it."

Fair enough. Because amid all the unadulterated joy, the deep emotional scars remain just beneath the joyous surface. That Jets logo covered countless broken hearts. As one woman standing at Portage and Main was heard to utter: "The tears are still on the pavement."

Chris Mackie was in his early 20s when the team left town. His indoctrination began with $7 tickets bought at McDonald's, and

Three-year-old Dylan Bridge and his brother Aiden, 6, practise their hockey skills during the celebrations at The Forks.

Katerina Moore (left) and her friend Alisha Long jump for joy after running into each other while celebrating the return of the NHL.

Amid all the unadulterated joy, the deep emotional scars remain just beneath the joyous surface. 'The tears are still on the pavement'

the seats were "the nosebleeds of the nosebleeds."

Years later, Mackie, an admitted hockey nerd, founded a website called Manitoba Mythbusters.com, dedicated to breaking down NHL economics and the potential return of the NHL to Winnipeg. When his dream finally came true, the manufacturing engineer was parked at the celebration at The Forks, decked out in a Jets ball cap and an Atlanta Thrashers jersey.

Yet even while standing at ground zero among the revelling masses, Mackie could easily summon the despair in seeing his team wither before his eyes.

"At that age, you're still in love with it," he explained. "But it was this strong feeling of helplessness. As my mother passed away with terminal cancer and we could see the end coming... it was very much how the Jets left. You loved it, you poured your heart and soul into it. And there was absolutely nothing you can do. That's about the closest I could come to (describing) it.

"God rest her soul that she's not mad at me for equating her with a hockey team, but she would understand what it meant to me."

Too much? Winnipeg-based psychologist Cal Botterill once noted: "If you look at it historically, people say hockey is like a religion. It's bigger than that. Because it's a thing that crosses all faiths — Jewish, Christian, Muslim... they all love hockey."

And precious few adored the Jets more than Mackie. During the doomed team's final lame-duck season in 1995-1996, he attended a handful of games and still remembers paying his last respects at the old Winnipeg Arena.

"I knew it would be my last game," he said. "It was like I couldn't even sit through it. I was thinking, 'What am I doing here?' It was a horrible existence. But the really sad thing was everybody in the city was going through it. It's not just a personal loss. It's everyone losing it at the same time. In some ways, I guess misery loves company, but it didn't offer any solace to anyone.

"The Jets' funeral was stark. It was as real as anything I could imagine. It's like I've been on pause for so long I really don't want to accept this. This has been going on for so long, the feeling of numbness. Too many highs and too many lows on the roller-coaster."

Imagine being spurned, crushed, then teased so often you've lost count. And hope. That's a Winnipeg NHL fan. That's Julie Klassen, sitting quietly with her husband, Randy, watching the mob gather at The Forks, donning a pin that reads, "I Helped Save the Jets," from the rally at The Forks on May 17, 1995.

How much did Klassen donate? "One hundred dollars, I think," she replied. "We thought the team would stay. We thought it would make a difference."

It didn't, of course. All the king's horses and all the king's men...

The Klassens didn't watch NHL hockey for years in the wake of the Jets' death. OK, maybe a few playoff games. They weren't alone. Neither did Hildahl, who explained: "It was more a sense of losing the NHL. It took me a long time to pay attention again."

Hell hath no fury like a woman scorned? Well, that woman must have been a Winnipeg Jets fan.

To this day, in fact, the NHL commissioner who presided over the demise of the Jets is a lightning rod for derision on the city's streets. Say Gary Bettman and spit. Buy the T-shirt.

In Manitoba, Bettman was symbolic of the NHL's rejection of its roots and its fans. It all went south when Bettman, a New York lawyer who rose through the ranks at the National Basketball Association, became NHL commissioner in 1993. That's when attempts to establish the game in southern, non-traditional markets began in earnest. To Canadians in general, and Winnipeggers specifically, Bettman is the Grinch Who Stole Hockey.

No sooner had Mark Chipman triumphantly declared the NHL's return than Bettman, who had jetted in for the announcement, pointedly stated to the gathered media: "Unless the fans support the franchise, it isn't going to work."

Really? You mean like in Phoenix? In Atlanta? In Miami?

Moose season-ticket holders had first dibs and took 7,158 seats. When the remaining 5,800 season tickets went on sale to the general public — with an unusual ask of three- to five-year commitments costing upwards of $25,000 — they sold out in less time than a minor penalty. Within 90 seconds, all 5,800 were gone. True North Sports & Entertainment capped the waiting list at 8,000.

WE WILL NEVER FORGET

WINNIPEG Jets

GOOD BYE AND GOOD LUCK

About 15,000 gathered at the Winnipeg Arena to say goodbye to the Jets in May 1995.

Emotionally, it was an awakening. Psychologically, it was empowering. The Little City That Couldn't, did

Somebody was breaking into the kids' piggy banks again.

The sellout, while almost instantaneous, was no accident. Wohlgemuth, for example, got wind two years before that if the NHL ever returned, Manitoba Moose season-ticket holders would get first dibs. So the agriculture sales rep bought two, just in case. "We didn't use them very much," he said. "I only went to about half the games, maybe a third."

On the Friday morning after the Announcement, Wohlgemuth, following True North's online instructions, bought four season tickets in the lower bowl at exactly 9 a.m. "without any stress." The price tag: $14,000 per season, with a four-year commitment.

Ingenuity was a must for the less fortunate, who had to anxiously wait until noon on Saturday. Chuck Duboff managed to score a half-season-ticket package for a group of eight. One of them lives in Cochrane, Alta., and plans to travel to Winnipeg for games. It wasn't a fluke. Duboff's friend, Geoff Brooks, was entrusted with the responsibility of navigating True North's Drive to 13,000 website when the clock struck 12.

"Geoff practised all day (Friday). That's all he did," Duboff said. He got on the site, practised going through all the steps that take you through the order form. And when 12 o'clock hit, he recognized all the pages and — click, click, click, click, click — he was forwarded to the page that said the order was there.

"And then I got an email at 12:11 with giant letters saying, 'CONGRATULATIONS! WE DID IT!' and I let out a scream I'm sure was heard right across the city."

Indeed, the entire week — from the official announcement, to the organic, chaotic celebrations, to the record sellout — was a release.

The city was on a hair-trigger. Ten days earlier, a Toronto columnist had reported — prematurely, as it turned out — the deal was done. True North denied it and so did the NHL, but late that night there were about 50 people, many in Winnipeg Jets jerseys, at Portage and Main chanting "Go, Jets, Go."

This time, it was real. Emotionally, it was an awakening. Psychologically, it was empowering. The Little City That Couldn't, did.

Izzy Asper, chairman of CanWest Global Communications, and Winnipeg mayor Susan Thompson in May 1995 when it became clear the Jets could really leave town.

It was an explosion of pent-up hope and frustration incubated in a place that had mourned for 15 winters — a place that has survived its relative isolation, its harsh environment and its own inferiority complex and collective desire not to be known as a minor-league city the NHL left behind.

Since 1996, in many ways, Winnipeg was a city drowning in regrets. When billionaire Izzy Asper's 11th-hour efforts to cobble together an ownership group to purchase the team from owner Barry Shenkarow failed in 1995, his youngest son, David, vividly recalls walking out of the Winnipeg Arena after the last game ruefully thinking, "What have we done?"

"Look, nothing is going to be easy here, OK?" David Asper

expanded. "Our weather is crappy. We have bugs that harass us all summer long. We've got floods. We don't have oil. Nothing's going to come easy here. But up until that point, we'd done pretty well. I don't want to equate the Jets to the other major milestones in our history, but we had a serious challenge and we didn't meet it.

"So the day after was not so much for me that it was over and the team was leaving, it was that we had kind of betrayed all the things that got us to this point, all the things that we'd overcome."

Winnipeg didn't just lose a hockey team. It lost history. It lost prestige. It lost civic pride. It lost Keith Tkachuk.

"I always argued at the time that there was an intrinsic value, that maybe we stuck out our chests a little bit more," said Stuart

Murray, who was heavily involved in attempts to save the Jets before later becoming leader of the provincial Conservative party from 2000 to 2006. "That when you turned to the sports pages anywhere in the world, there would be Winnipeg with Los Angeles, New York, Toronto, Montreal. We were a player in the premier hockey league in the world.

"I thought it gave us a sense of ownership and a sense of pride that we, as Winnipeggers, could play in the same sandbox as our friends from Alberta or our friends from Ontario or south of the border. We played in that sandbox. We deserved to be in that sandbox. When it gets taken away..."

There are tears on the pavement. Then one day, those tears are washed away by spilled beer and champagne. The bitter taste gets washed away, too.

The regrets are exorcised. The dead are resurrected.

Mark Olson cried the day the Jets left. He cried the day they came back.

"It just overwhelmed me, tears running down my face," said Olson, who — and how Winnipeg is this? — was a curler who organized a social that raised almost $250,000 toward saving the Jets in May of 1995. "It was an amazing feeling."

But the Jets were gone. Olson gave his social money to the Winnipeg Children's Hospital. But he never stopped pining for his team. And when the new Winnipeg Jets play their first home game on Oct. 9 against the Montreal Canadiens, Olson plans to be there with his 80-year-old dad, Albert. Just like the old days at the arena.

"I was there for the opening of the NHL," he said. "I was there for the last game of the NHL. And I want to be at the first game back."

But back on May 31, Olson was casting a wistful gaze over the youngsters like Will Stangeland partying like it was, well, '99.

"We saw the Gretzkys, we saw the Selannes, we saw the Lemieuxs," Olson said. Now, he said, it was time for the young fans to see the current superstars. "Now this is going to be their chance. This is going to be a great opportunity for them.

"You can just feel the excitement. They see the Hawerchuk jerseys in the closet. They've heard the stories. But now they're

Winnipeg didn't just lose a hockey team. It lost history. It lost prestige. It lost civic pride. It lost Keith Tkachuk

Jets forward Keith Tkachuk during a game against the Buffalo Sabres in January 1996.

going to see the Ovechkins and the Crosbys. This could be something that 50 years from now, people will remember this day. I mean, how many chances in your life do you get to experience something as unique as this? Look around. When is the last time you've seen so many smiling faces in Winnipeg?"

Well, since Olson asked, there were a few times. In fact, when Andrew Lima and his buddy Brad Gebhardt found their way to the corner of Portage and Main on that glorious and miserable May evening, they were following in the footsteps of their shinny-mad forefathers who had come before to that same piece of real estate. Just as Mark Chipman wasn't the first salesman from Winnipeg to literally reach for the hockey stars.

And perhaps that explained the cosmic tsunami of emotions; why grown men cried and teenage girls gushingly celebrated the return of something they'd never seen. It's why everybody — six times what the arena could have held — was at that last Jets game. It wasn't just that the NHL had returned. It was an awakening of collective memory.

The Winnipeg Jets weren't history anymore. They were reborn. And a new generation of fans and their children were about to experience the hockey fairy tales their mothers and fathers told them in reverent tones.

Hull's triumphant signing. Ulf and Anders. A baby-faced Hawerchuk. The year when Teemu scored 76 as a rookie. The night Dave Ellett blew the roof off the old barn. Oh, and don't forget, Gretzky sucks.

It's a story almost 40 years in the making, rife with all the elements of a Greek tragedy, only rewritten with a happy ending. Or, more fittingly, a new beginning.

Where to start? Why, at Portage and Main, of course.

High-fiving at Portage and Main May 19, 2011 after a false news report that a deal had been struck.

DAVID LIPNOWSKI WINNIPEG FREE PRESS

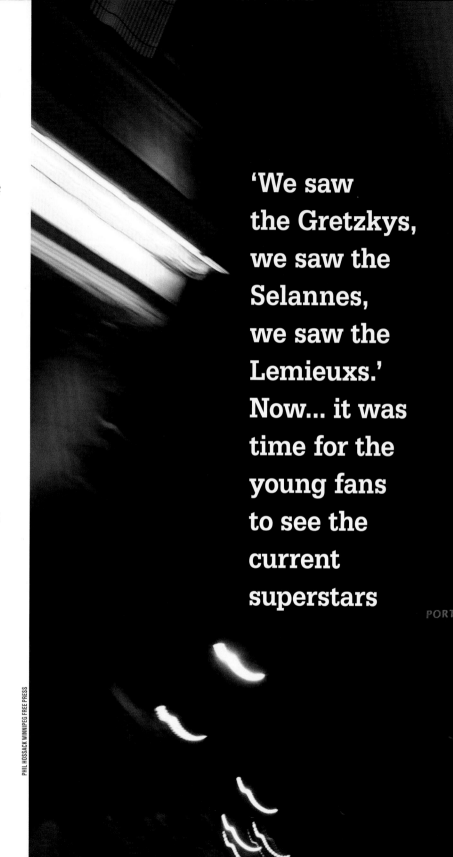

PHIL HOSSACK WINNIPEG FREE PRESS

'We saw the Gretzkys, we saw the Selannes, we saw the Lemieuxs.' Now... it was time for the young fans to see the current superstars

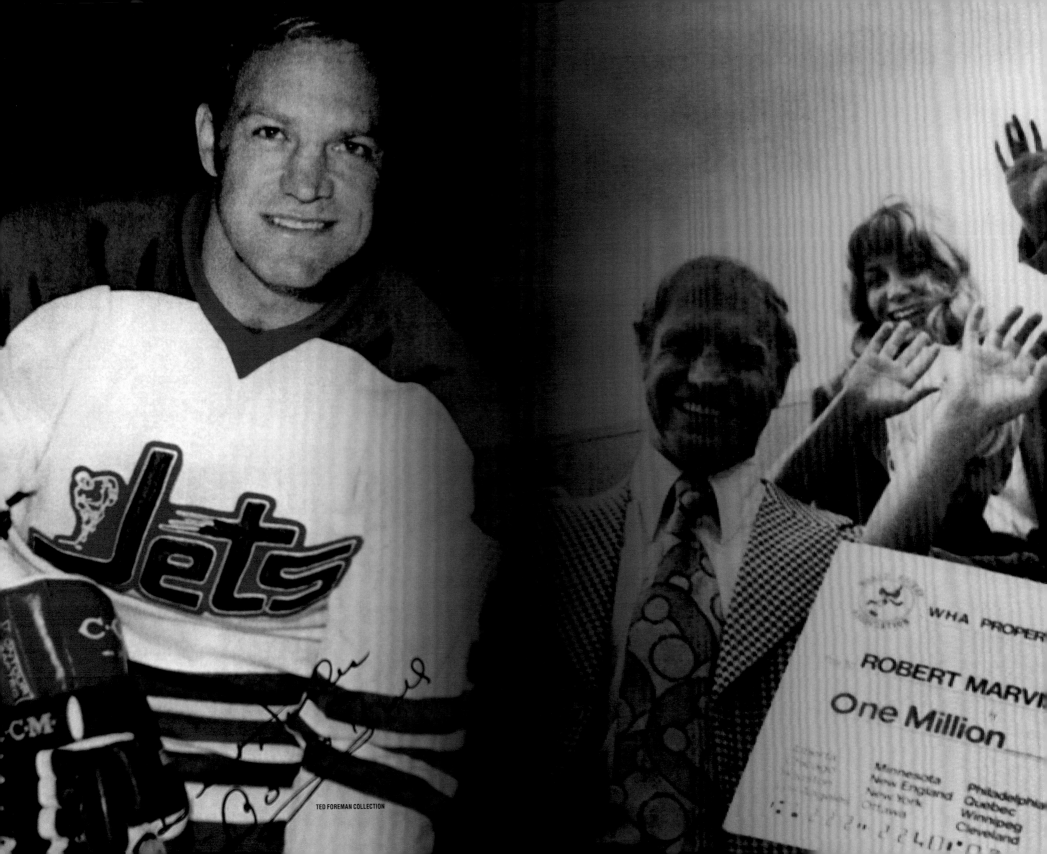

WHA PROPER

ROBERT MARVI

One Million

Minnesota   Philadelphia
New England   Quebec
New York   Winnipeg
Ottawa   Cleveland

CHAPTER TWO:

The Golden Jet

IN the blue skies over Winnipeg that gorgeous June morning in 1972, perhaps the world's greatest hockey player was grinning like a thief, sipping on champagne as though it was out of the Stanley Cup. The Transair charter plane was filled with dreamers who had just made Bobby Hull rich.

The destination was Portage and Main. The revolution was underway. An oversized cheque for $1 million was on the plane. So was Bob Verdi, a somewhat bewildered 27-year-old beat writer for the *Chicago Tribune*.

Bobby Hull holds a cheque worth $1 million after signing a World Hockey Association contract with the Winnipeg Jets on June 27, 1972.

Hatskin had just pulled off one of the biggest coups in professional sports history, luring Hull away from the National Hockey League's Chicago Black Hawks

Verdi couldn't stop thinking, "Is this really happening?" The reporter cast a glance over at a large, former professional football player with silver hair who was bouncing about the plane as though it were literally passing through cloud nine. Ben Hatskin was beaming.

"He was smiling like a pig in, you know," Verdi recalled, "and rightfully so."

Hatskin had just pulled off one of the biggest coups in professional sports history, luring Hull away from the National Hockey League's Chicago Black Hawks (who sported a two-word moniker until 1986) and at the same time serving notice that the newborn World Hockey Association was entering the world kicking and screaming. Perhaps even he couldn't believe it, or fully comprehend what he'd just done.

It was a story some 60 years in the making. Hatskin's parents had emigrated from the Jewish settlement of Proproisk, in modern-day Belarus, loading their belongings on a horse-drawn wagon for a gruelling journey to Liverpool, England, where they had purchased passage for their new life in North America. But the rain in Eastern Europe was especially heavy in that spring of 1912, and the muddy roads slowed them down. By the time Lazer (Louis) Hatskin and his wife, Annie Cohen, reached Liverpool, the RMS Titanic had sailed without them.

Forty years later, Nazi invaders annihilated Proproisk. The town's name was changed to Slavgorod, and in April 1986 it was heavily contaminated with radioactive fallout from the Chornobyl nuclear disaster.

So fate had a history of smiling on the Hatskins, who settled in Winnipeg's North End and founded a wooden-box company, later prospering with the manufacture of corrugated paper boxes.

Boxes. How ironic that their son, Benjamin, born in 1913, could never be kept in one.

Every Friday night, there was a family dinner and inevitably, Ben, his father and brother Rube would get into heated arguments over the family business. "It was a free-for-all," chuckled Hatskin's nephew, Ken Kronson.

Hatskin was a big kid. He took to football, earning a scholarship at the University of Oklahoma before toiling six years for the Winnipeg Blue Bombers as an offensive lineman. Not much for boxes, Hatskin owned a stable and had a yen for the track. He owned a downtown nightclub, the Town N' Country, that once booked an unknown 19-year-old singer named Barbra Streisand.

Friends called him "Fats."

Hatskin rolled large, too, always behind the wheel of a Cadillac, with his minder, Charlie Shepard, a former Bombers fullback, riding shotgun. His main source of revenue was as the largest distributor of jukeboxes on the Canadian Prairies. Word on the street was Hatskin was a bit of a mobster. It wasn't true, but Hatskin was vague about denying it.

More than anything, though, Ben Hatskin liked money and had a gift for producing the stuff. His father would force him to take violin lessons, but the adolescent balked. "Can you imagine a baby hippopotamus playing the fiddle?" Hatskin said later. The only music he loved, Ben boasted, "is played on a cash register."

Exhibit A: In 1967, he founded the Junior Jets, who competed in the old Western Canada Hockey League, playing against the likes of Bobby Clarke's Flin Flon Bombers. Well, one year the Jets and Bombers were to meet in a best-of-seven playoff. The old Winnipeg Arena was jammed to the rafters. So, boom, Benny made it a best-of-nine. Nobody complained.

When Hatskin announced his intentions of throwing in with the schemers and dreamers behind the rebellious WHA with a franchise called the Jets, the *Winnipeg Tribune* assigned the new beat to 29-year-old Vic Grant. Years later, when Hatskin died in October 1990, Grant would serve as a pallbearer. But back in the spring of 1972, Grant would sit patiently outside Hatskin's office every morning waiting for an audience.

"He was an intimidating individual if you didn't know him," said Grant. "He was looked upon as a bit of a gangster. A lot of people thought he had connections to the Mafia. He had a reputation as a bit of a shady character, to put it politely. His exterior was loud and crass. He barked at people who had to scurry every which way when he wanted something. That's the image of Ben Hatskin as a tough, no-nonsense character. Ninety per cent of

it was reputation. You always wondered, but... "

Hatskin modelled himself after another brash character, Sonny Werblin, owner of the American Football League's New York Jets, who stunned the sports world in 1965 when he signed quarterback Joe Namath. Werblin owned a few nightclubs and loved the ponies, too. And by shelling out a then-astounding $427,000 to lure Namath out of the clutches of the establishment NFL, Werblin forever altered the course of professional sports history.

Hatskin was determined that his Jets were also going to carry a big shtick. The guy who grew up on Bannerman and Pritchard avenues was going to put Winnipeg on the proverbial map. He was going to be a contender, a gambler.

Ben Hatskin, pictured in 1989, founded the Junior Jets, of the Western Canadian Hockey League, in 1967.

Hull, left, with
Chicago Black
Hawks president
William Wirtz
during a ceremony
to retire his No. 9
Black Hawks jersey
in December 1983.

Besides, it's not as though Hatskin didn't have the audacity to get into the NHL from the beginning. Prior to the league's second expansion to Buffalo and Vancouver in 1970, he called then-NHL commissioner Clarence Campbell to kick the tires. Campbell told him he'd need a rink that sat 16,000 and a $7.2-million entry fee. Benny had neither.

So when the World Hockey Association was hatched, Hatskin jumped for the franchise fee of $25,000.

"I figured it was maybe the only chance our city would ever have to go major-league in any sport," he said. "Besides, we had something to prove to the disbelievers, who were, by far, in the majority."

Oh, there were doubters, and for good reason. At first, Hatskin was widely considered a barker without a circus. Sure, he loved food. He'd talk about one meal for two months and was known to carry a wrapped corned beef sandwich around in his pocket for a "midday snack." But the consensus was this time Hatskin had bitten off much more than even he could chew. Or the cynics could swallow.

"How would you like to see Bobby Hull play in Winnipeg?" Hatskin first teased in October of 1971. "Don't laugh. It's not beyond the realm of possibility."

More than once, Grant would ask Hatskin, "This Bobby Hull stuff — it's bullshit, right?"

Later, Hatskin would say, "I know that months ago, when I first mentioned the Winnipeg Jets would try to sign Bobby Hull, everybody thought it was just a publicity stunt. But I was never more serious about anything in my life."

It's true. Hatskin had managed to persuade most of his fellow WHA owners to each throw $100,000 into the kitty. The plan was audaciously simple: Sign Hull for a million bucks and the powerful left-winger would become hockey's Broadway Joe. Hull would fill their arenas and instantly legitimize a league that was going to war against the monopoly of the smug NHL dictators.

Indeed, the late 1960s and early 1970s were defined by rebellion. The AFL begat the WHA. In Major League Baseball, players were revolting against an archaic and doomed system of lifetime contracts. It was the birth of free agency and long hair.

Yet NHL owners had grown used to paying even a player of Hull's tenure and status — he was 33 and, at the time, the second-highest goal scorer in NHL history, trailing only Gordie Howe — barely into six figures. Hull was in the last year of a contract that paid him $150,000 a year. He wanted $250,000 from the Black Hawks' tight-fisted owners Arthur Wirtz and his son, Bill.

Hull's ears were open. He was even willing to listen to a big talker from a small, frozen Canadian city whose "team" was nothing but a name on a piece of paper. Reasoned Hatskin: "There are only three or four superstars in hockey. All but Hull were tied up. He was our trump card."

Meanwhile, the Black Hawks and the NHL were only helping Hatskin's cause. They were almost indignant at the notion of a rival league, especially one with franchises in outposts like Winnipeg, Calgary and Ottawa. Besides, who would want to put professional hockey in places like Phoenix (Roadrunners) and Miami (Screaming Eagles) anyway? Please.

The Wirtz family was going to call the WHA's bluff. Go ahead, Bobby, sign with the "Winnipeg Jets." Here's our offer, take it or leave. Oh, we hear the winters in Manitoba are gorgeous.

So it was that in May of 1972, as Verdi was minding his own business at his home in Chicago, the phone rang. It was Hull. "I might have something for you," No. 9 said.

Verdi raced to Hull's home in a suburb called Glen Ellyn and took a seat at the kitchen table. As Hull spoke, his seven-year-old son, Brett, was hanging on Verdi's pant leg. Hull talked, and Verdi took notes.

It was a Friday afternoon. The headline in Saturday's *Tribune* read, "Hull: If Winnipeg pays me, I'm gone."

The you-know hit the fan. But the skepticism remained. Said Verdi: "There was still a sense that the Black Hawks wouldn't let Bobby go. It's crazy. Why would he go to Winnipeg? Why would he go anywhere?"

For cash, apparently. Winter in Winnipeg isn't the only thing that's cold and hard.

The Black Hawks blinked, offering Hull close to his original

Roy Thomson

demand of $250,000 a season. But there was Hatskin again, telling Hull his million-dollar offer was genuine. And up front.

The NHL tall foreheads, at least those with some vision, were getting nervous. Jack Kent Cooke owned the Los Angeles Kings, a team that had just finished its fifth season on the West Coast, where the NHL wanted to grow its game in a sunny climate. Cooke was an expatriate Canadian who, back in 1936, met a fellow young mogul-in-the-making named Roy Thomson, who hired him to run a radio station in Stratford, Ont. The two men became partners in 1941. Thomson's grandson, David, was born in 1957. The NHL would hear from him later, too.

Jack Kent Cooke

Cooke was fretting that Hull was about to bolt for the WHA's financially greener pastures. And he was urging the Wirtzes to get off their wallets. Since Cooke also owned the NBA's Los Angeles Lakers and the Wirtzes owned the Chicago Bulls, he made a bold proposal: He would trade Kareem Abdul-Jabbar for Bobby Hull. "If you don't sign him, I will," Cooke implored.

"I'm not sure how serious he (Cooke) was," Verdi said, "but he was wise enough to know that if Hull left, it was going to cost the NHL a fortune."

Hull's million-dollar
smile June 27, 1972.
(Left) Jets owner
Ben Hatskin.

Next thing Verdi knows, it's the early afternoon of June 27, 1972 and he's on a plane to Winnipeg, having just left St. Paul, where Hull officially signed for his certified million-dollar bonus to avoid Canada's more stringent tax laws.

Hull turned to wife Joanne and said, "That's the longest she's ever handled one of my cheques without spending it."

Grant was on the plane, too, along with a horde of reporters from across the country Hatskin had invited to witness the historic triumph. "It was a whirlwind, a Hollywood-type atmosphere," Grant recalled.

The forecast was for rain. But the only thing that fell out of the sky that day was the Golden Jet, who jumped into a 1934 Rolls-Royce for the waiting parade along Wellington Avenue, south on St. James Street, east down Portage and up Broadway to the Fort Garry Hotel.

Word of Hull's signing spread through the city streets like the flood of 1950. Fans by the thousands made their way to the intersection. For many, it was surreal. Bobby Hull? Playing for Winnipeg?!

Yet here was Bobby Hull, standing at Portage and Main with another giant cheque. This one was for $2.75 million, spread over 10 years. The traffic was backed up for blocks in three directions. Gawkers stood on their cars to catch a glimpse of Hull flashing his million-dollar smile. "It was like scoring my 51st goal," he said.

The immediate reaction: part disbelief, part bedlam.

Ted Foreman was a financial adviser who would eventually end up handling Hull's windfall. But like most hockey fans, he had trouble believing his own eyes.

"Are you kidding? Bobby Hull coming to Winnipeg? What a bunch of bull," Foreman said of the prevailing attitudes of the day. "No damn athlete is worth $1 million. That'll never happen. This was the stuff that was floating around. Then all of a sudden, bingo, this blond guy is at Portage and Main."

A week later, Hatskin's office received a bill in the mail for $2.40. It was from a woman whose taxi got stuck in the traffic jam and she blamed Benny. "For half an hour," the *Free Press* dutifully reported, "the only thing that moved was the meter."

'First of all, nobody believed Winnipeg could go out and sign arguably the greatest player at that time. That was almost unheard of. For me as a player, as soon as Bobby signed, that was my insurance policy'

— Joe Daley

Hatskin displays the million-dollar contract at Portage and Main. Bobby Hull donned a Jets jersey for the occasion.

Winnipeg was in ecstasy. Chicago was in shock. The grin on Hatskin's mug stretched as wide as the Trans-Canada. The NHL pretended not to care.

"In the same light as if he (Hull) had died, broken his leg or retired," sniffed the crusty owner of the Toronto Maple Leafs, Harold Ballard. "We would have had to get along without him if any of those things had happened."

But as Ballard and his NHL brethren would soon come to understand, Hull was just the beginning. Household hockey names like Bernie Parent, J.C. Tremblay, Derek Sanderson, Ted Green and Gerry Cheevers would follow. Stars, let alone superstars, no longer played for $150,000 a year. Cooke was right. Hull left, and it cost the NHL a fortune.

And for the less notable who feared being the NHL blackballing them after defecting to the unknown quantity of the WHA, the relief was palpable. One of those thousands of faces in the mob the day Hull became a Jet belonged to a journeyman netminder named Joe Daley.

Daley had signed with the Jets just days before Hull, doubling the wage he earned the previous season as a backup with the Detroit Red Wings. Daley wasn't just a Jet, he was a Winnipegger, born and raised in East Kildonan before making his way in professional hockey, bouncing around the minors from Memphis to Pittsburgh to San Francisco to Baltimore.

Now Daley was home at age 28 and playing big-time hockey for the princely sum of $60,000. Check that. Playing hockey with Bobby Hull in his hometown for sixty large.

"It was almost unbelievable," Daley said. "First of all, nobody believed Winnipeg could go out and sign arguably the greatest player at that time. That was almost unheard of. For me as a player, as soon as Bobby signed, that was my insurance policy."

Daley would go on to become the only Jet to play all seven WHA seasons in Winnipeg. Today, he runs a sports collectibles store not far from where the old Winnipeg Arena once stood. Without question, he remembers signing with the Jets as the best decision of his life.

The Golden Jet — Bobby Hull — addresses the crowd at Portage and Main after signing his WHA contract with the Jets.

CANCENTRAL CARD & SUPPLY

"Having left as a 19-year-old to pursue my career and then get a chance to come back as a 28-year-old and play at home... that in itself was a dream," Daley recalled. "So it was a very special time, not only for the fans, but a guy like myself. It was meaningful."

Daley wasn't alone. Ab McDonald, another Winnipegger, had just finished his 17th NHL season, an illustrious career that included winning Stanley Cups four straight years — three with the Montreal Canadiens and one with Bobby Hull in Chicago in 1961.

McDonald and Hull went back even farther to their junior days with the St. Catharines Teepees. At age 36, with the stitches and mileage of more than 800 games behind him, McDonald came home with less fanfare than his old teammate.

"How much did I get?" McDonald blurted, when asked if Hatskin was just as generous to him as to Hull. "Not $1 million, I'll tell ya. I was just happy to get a team back (in Winnipeg) and play here."

Posterity will record that old Ab McDonald would score the first goal in Winnipeg Jets history in the team's inaugural game, on the road against the New York Raiders (a 6-4 Jets victory) on Oct. 12, 1972. McDonald doesn't recall the goal, specifically, but he'll remember the night forever.

Back in Winnipeg, only two hours later, McDonald's wife, Pat, gave birth to the couple's fifth child, Kristina. Since Dad was busy, a neighbour drove Pat McDonald to the hospital. Another neighbour drove her back home.

Yes, it was a different time. In 1972, the Climatic Research Unit opened to study the effect of greenhouse gases on climate change. Jack Nicklaus passed Arnold Palmer as the all-time money leader on the PGA Tour. The first episode of *The Price is Right* aired on television. Lester B. Pearson died. Martin Brodeur was born.

And Bobby Hull signed with the Winnipeg Jets, and the world took notice.

The American sports writer Shirley Povich, in a column that ran in newspapers across North America on June 30, observed of Hull's arrival in Winnipeg: "A likely story that did not appear to have even the saving grace of sounding merely specious has evolved as a story of staggering truth."

"Fats" had fooled them all.

Bobby Hull,
No. 9, winds
up his feared
slapshot in a
game against
the Phoenix
Roadrunners.

The Jets played the Soviet Union's national team in Winnipeg on Jan. 5, 1978. Here, Bobby Hull takes up position in front of Soviet goalie Vladislav Tretiak.

Thommie Bergman, No. 2, Bobby Hull, No. 9, and Lars-Erik Sjöberg, No. 4, play the Birmingham Bulls on Nov. 16 1977.

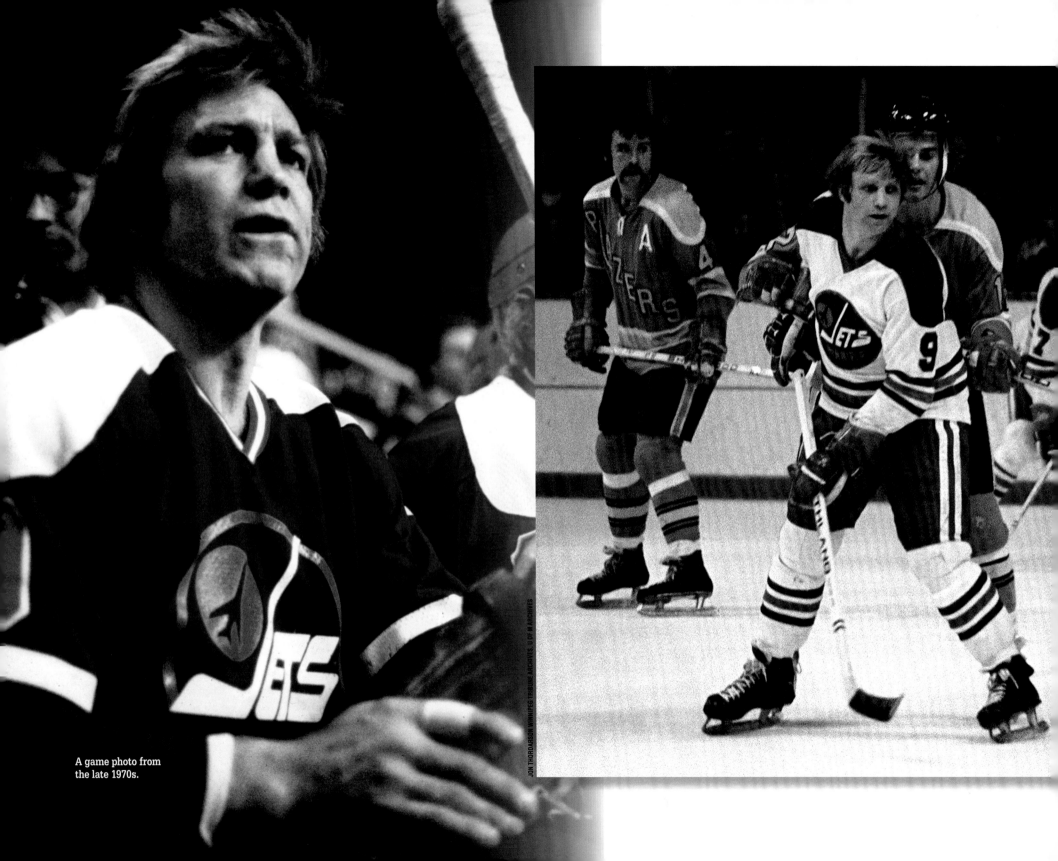

A game photo from the late 1970s.

"He (Hatskin) was the right guy at the right time," Daley said. "Everything else is history."

When Hull signed, Phil Esposito whistled: "A million dollars? Oy vey!" Back in Winnipeg, Jets teammate Bob Woytowich, who had earlier bolted from the Los Angeles Kings, smirked and told reporters: "I've seen Hull play. I think he can help." And *Free Press* hockey writer Reyn Davis cheerfully scribbled: "You could hardly wait for winter."

But more than winter was coming. So much more. After all, who could have known what the future would hold? Or how that single event in time would forever alter fates? Like Lazer Hatskin arriving late for the Titanic.

The Winnipeg Jets were born that day in June 1972 and life for Winnipeg hockey fans, for generations to come, was going to be linked directly back to the exact moment Bobby Hull stopped traffic at Portage and Main. For better or worse.

After all, without Hull, what would have become of the infant Jets? And didn't Ulf and Anders come to Winnipeg just to play on the same line? And without the WHA Jets, would the NHL ever have darkened the city's door in 1979? The what-ifs are endless.

But there was no turning back. The future awaited, unwritten, a clean sheet of ice.

Paths would be crossed. Lives would change.

Who knew? Not long before the impossible dream of a Russian immigrant's son took root in Winnipeg, in 1970, half a world away in Helsinki, Finland, a woman named Liisa Viitaten gave birth to twin boys. She called one of her sons Paavo.

The other she named Teemu.

But there was no turning back. The future awaited, unwritten, a clean sheet of ice

The Jets play the Philadelphia Blazers on April 4, 1975.

Hull gives fellow Jet Peter Sullivan a look during playoff
action against the New England Whalers on May 20, 1978.

Captain Lars-Erik Sjöberg
hoists the Avco Cup after the
Jets beat the Edmonton Oilers
7-3 on May 20, 1979.

JON THORDARSON WINNIPEG TRIBUNE, U OF M ARCHIVES

JUNE 27, 1972

The Golden Jet Bobby Hull — signs a 10-year contract with the Jets, with the other WHA owners chipping in, for a total of $2.75 million. The 33-year-old had just completed his 15th season with the Chicago Black Hawks and, at the time, stood second to Gordie Howe in NHL career scoring.

"My main concern now isn't the bonuses," Hull says at a news conference after arriving from the airport in a Rolls-Royce. "It is getting the WHA off the ground. I don't think the Black Hawks thought I was serious — or the WHA was serious — about this."

OCT. 12, 1972

The WHA Jets play their first game — minus Bobby Hull, whose debut is delayed while he battles the Black Hawks in court — and skate to a 6-4 win over the New York Raiders in front of 6,273 at Madison Square Garden. Pepe Bordeleau paces the Jets with four goals and an assist. *Free Press* headline that day: "Jets Are A Hit On Broadway"

OCT. 15, 1972

The Jets — still minus Hull, fall 5-2 to the Alberta Oilers in their home opener.

NOV. 8, 1972 —

Hull makes his Jets and WHA debut — after a judge rules against the Black Hawks' injunction — in a 3-2 loss to the Quebec Nordiques at Le Colisée. Hull picks up his first point, an assist on a goal by Danny Johnson, with five seconds left in the game and receives a standing ovation when he first steps on the ice.

MAY 6, 1973

The inaugural season — of the WHA ends with the New England Whalers knocking off the Jets 9-6 to capture the first Avco Cup in five games.

That first campaign features the Jets, Alberta Oilers, Chicago Cougars, Houston Aeros, Los Angeles Sharks and Minnesota Fighting Saints in the Western Division while the Cleveland Crusaders, New England Whalers, New York Raiders, Ottawa Nationals, Philadelphia Blazers and Quebec Nordiques comprise the Eastern Division.

MAY 3, 1974

The Jets — becoming the first North American team to truly mine Europe for talent, sign two Swedish players, Anders Hedberg and Ulf Nilsson, who would form an instant chemistry with Hull on the Hot Line. Twenty days later, defenceman Lars-Erik Sjöberg is also signed.

FEB. 14, 1975

Hull takes a pass from Nilsson — and beats Houston Aeros goaltender Ron Grahame for a hat trick and his 50th goal in 50 games — tying a record set by Montreal Canadiens legend Rocket Richard in 1944-45.

"Only a strong man could

ever do such a thing. Hull, if he wasn't so weak, he'd have 60 by now!" teases Aeros legend Gordie Howe after the game.

APRIL 6, 1975

The Jets miss the playoffs — for the only time in their WHA existence, but in their regular-season finale at the Winnipeg Arena, Hull scores his 77th goal to break Phil Esposito's 1970-71 record of 76.

"When no one else has scored as many goals in one season, it's just a great feeling," Hull tells *Free Press* hockey writer Reyn Davis. "But I could never have done it without the fantastic workload of Anders (Hedberg) and Ulf (Nilsson). The record is a credit to the three of us."

MAY 27, 1976

The Jets hammer the Houston Aeros 9-1 — at the Winnipeg Arena to capture their first Avco Cup championship. The win is significant because the Jets not only become the first Canadian team to win the Avco Cup, but because the team's free-flowing style of play is the opposite of the Philadelphia Flyers' — dubbed the Broad Street Bullies after grinding and pounding their way to back-to-back Stanley Cup championships in 1974-75.

"The most important thing of all is that it's now been proven that Canadian-style hockey and Winnipeg-style hockey wins championships," proclaimed Anders Hedberg, who had 13 goals in 13 playoff games.

FEB. 6, 1977

...ders Hedberg, dubbed the ...edish Express — climbs off ...e trainer's table during a 6-4 ...n over the Calgary Cowboys ...d, despite a broken rib and ...e knee, scores three times ...the last his 51st goal in 47 ...mes — to break the record of ...in 50 set by Richard and tied ...Hull.

...edberg is one of the greatest ...ht-wingers I've ever seen," ...s Calgary head coach Joe ...ozier. "And that's a compli-...ent because I feel I've seen ...most all of the great ones."

MAY 26, 1977 —

...e Nordiques — backstopped ...goaltender Richard Brodeur ...d led by Serge Bernier and ...al Cloutier, knock off the Jets ...2 at Le Colisée in Quebec ...ty in the seventh game of the ...co Cup final.

JAN. 5, 1978

...their fourth meeting of the ...ason — and after three losses ...games played in Japan, ...e Jets knock off the Soviet ...ational Team 5-3 at the Win-...peg Arena, becoming the only ...b team to defeat the eight-...me world champions. Hull ...ds the Jets with three goals ...d an assist and proclaims ...th a grin: "I'm not as good ...I once was, but I'm as good ...ce as I ever was" but is quick ...praise the work of goaltender ...e Daley. It is one of the great-...t moments in Jets history, but ...s seen by very few outside ...Winnipeg — the CBC opts to ...levise a game between the St. ...uis Blues and the sixth-place ...ssian team, Spartak. Spartak ...ns 2-1.

MAY 22, 1978

The Jets complete a spec-tacular season — that saw them post 50 wins and have four players score more than 100 points — Ulf Nilsson, 126; Anders Hedberg, 122; Bobby Hull, 117 and WHA Rookie of the Year Kent Nilsson, 107 — by beating the New England Whalers 5-3 at the Winnipeg Arena to win their second Avco Cup championship.

MARCH 22, 1979

After months of haggling — the NHL agrees to a merger plan with the WHA that will see Winnipeg, Edmonton, Hartford and Quebec added the following season.

MAY 20, 1979

The final year of the WHA concludes with the Jets — minus Ulf and Anders after they signed with the New York Rangers but bolstered by the additions of former Houston Aeros Rich Preston, Morris Lukowich, Terry Ruskowski and Paul Terbenche after that franchise folded and goaltender Gary 'Suitcase' Smith — win-ning the final Avco Cup in six games over Wayne Gretzky and the Edmonton Oilers.

John Ferguson, who replaces Rudy Pilous as the GM in November, makes another dra-matic management move by fir-ing Larry Hillman in March and hiring his pal Tom McVie, one of the funniest men in hockey but hardly with a glowing re-sumé. McVie had been fired by the Washington Capitals.

"I was standing on my front porch for five months," McVie told Ed Willes in his book on the WHA, *The Rebel League.* "It got to the point where the mail-man crossed the street when he saw me standing there. The first two days (after being fired by the Caps) everyone in hock-ey called to sympathize with me. Then the calls stopped. I'd check my phone to make sure there was still a dial tone."

Interestingly, Ron Anderson, scored the first-ever WHA goal as a member of the Alberta Oil-ers in 1972, and Dave Semenko, an Oiler, scores the last in a 7-3 loss to the Jets in the final.

THE WHA YEARS
(1972-79)

JON THORDARSON WINNIPEG TRIBUNE, U OF M ARCHIVES

CHAPTER THREE:

The Jets Take Off

ANOTHER flight, this time into the heart of Gotham.

All aboard for Northwest Orient Flight 215, now sailing high above Niagara Falls, bound for New York. The date is Oct. 11, 1972, on the eve of the Jets' first wobbly strides in the World Hockey Association and a date with the equally embryonic New York Raiders at Madison Square Garden.

Billy "Sudsy" Sutherland, the centreman, looked around the plane: "We're a bunch of ragamuffins," he thought.

The stewardess, which is what a flight attendant was called in 1972, thought: "I've seen worse."

Lars-Erik Sjöberg, Dave Dunn and Ted Green (from left) on the Jets' bench, May 20, 1978.

'Kid, if I had legs like that, I'd walk on my hands'

— Coach Ed Dorohoy to Brian Cadle

She had, too. Flight 215's last passenger list had been the Oakland Athletics, the 1972 version. The Reggie Jackson, Vida Blue, Rollie Fingers, all-anti-establishment Charlie O. Finley Oakland Athletics. They made this band of nervous hockey players look angelic by comparison.

Joe Daley, the goaltender, was munching on a bag of peanuts, reading a Raiders program. Fellow netminder Ernie Wakely, a 31-year-old out of Flin Flon, was reading F. Lee Bailey's *The Defense Never Rests*. Neither would Wakely, who went on to play more WHA games than any other goaltender in league history.

Larry Hornung, a well-travelled defenceman who'd played just 48 NHL games in six years, was doing the crossword puzzle in the *New York Daily News*. Hornung, then 26, was about to have his career season on the Jets' blue-line. Centreman Wally Boyer, all 5-8 and 165 pounds of him, was from the tiny town of Cowan, Man. He was a white-knuckle flyer, too, peering out the window, muttering, "Only 93 miles to go."

Danny Johnson, Garth Rizzuto, Freeman "Duke" Asmundson and Steve Cuddie were playing four-handed crib. In 1974, Johnson, born in Winnipegosis, Man., would become the second captain in Jets history. Rizzuto, from Trail, B.C., was the first British Columbia-born player to score a goal for the expansion Vancouver Canucks in 1970. Asmundson, a rangy winger, was from Vita, Man. And Cuddie, 22, was a defenceman from Toronto who would lead the Jets in penalty minutes (121) in his only season in Winnipeg.

But the ragamuffin of the bunch was undoubtedly Winnipeg's own Brian Cadle, who the season before had been toiling in anonymity for the Des Moines Oak Leafs of the International Hockey League.

Just 23, Cadle had a mop top. In his team photo, he looked for all the world like the fifth Beatle.

Cadle was born and raised in Elmwood and was a first-generation instigator, a poor man's Eddie Shack.

"Couldn't skate," Cadle said in later years, rhyming off his non-gifts. "Couldn't shoot. I always tell people I tried harder than everyone else."

But Cadle feared nothing and no one. "I liked the bigger guys," he said. "I was afraid of the small, tough guys. But the bigger they were, I didn't care."

So why did Cadle become the Jets' first cult celebrity? Probably because he stood over 6-0 and weighed about 170 pounds, almost none of it below the waist. Cadle had legs so spindly that teammates used to rag him for not wearing shin pads, even though he had them on. Writers joked that if Cadle skated too fast, his legs might catch fire rubbing against each other.

Once, during his junior days, Cadle had just returned to his stall from the shower. Coach Ed Dorohoy looked at him and barked: "Kid, if I had legs like that, I'd walk on my hands."

Cadle had heard them all. But that didn't stop the Winnipeg crowds from chanting, "We Want Cadle! We Want Cadle!" in those early days, just to see what kind of havoc might ensue. The fans even had a name: "Cadle's Cronies."

The chants weren't a mystery to Cadle. "I know why," he said, years later. "Because the game was dull."

That was the Achilles heel of the WHA. For every Hull or Cheevers or ageless Gordie Howe, there were a dozen bladed foot soldiers — career minor-leaguers and misfits — who were the stuff of every roster. The rebel league was their ticket to the big leagues, even one that existed in an alternate, unpredictable universe, a distant neighbour to the storied, just-out-of-grasp NHL.

Cadle signed with the Jets for $15,000. He would have played for nothing, or a few grand more than his pay stub with the immortal Oak Leafs.

It looked like it would be a rough night in the Garden. The NHL had obtained an injunction in Philadelphia federal court, claiming Hull's contract and Bob Woytowich's were invalid. The Golden Jet couldn't even stand behind the bench.

No matter. Christian "Pepe" Bordeleau, who for years had been an anonymous spare part in the Montreal Canadiens system, scored four times, adding an assist, in a 6-4 Jets victory witnessed by a curious New York crowd of 6,300. *Tribune* reporter Vic Grant was there. "That night," he recalled, "we had the second-greatest hockey player in the world."

Canadian

WINNIPEG JETS
October 15, 1972

1	JOE DALEY
30	ERNIE WAKELY
2	BOB WOYTOWICH (A)
3	BOB ASH
4	JOE ZANUSSI
5	LARRY HORNUNG
6	STEVE CUDDIE
7	CHRIS BORDELEAU
8	WALLY BOYER
9	BOBBY HULL
10	BILL SUTHERLAND (A)
11	NORM BEAUDIN
12	DUNC ROUSSEAU
14	AB McDONALD (C)
15	GARTH RIZZUTO
16	JEAN GUY GRATTON
17	DANNY JOHNSON
18	CAL SWENSON
19	MILT BLACK
0	BRIAN CADLE
	DUKE ASMUNDSON

AL MANAGER—Annis Stukus
—Bobby Hull
NT COACH—Nick Mickoski
—Diarmid McVicar
NT—Steve Adamski

...that's the b

ALBERTA OILERS
October 15, 1972

1	KEN BROWN
30	JACK NORRIS
2	ROGER COTE
3	AL HAMILTON
4	BOB WALL
5	DOUG BARRIE
6	BOB FALKENBERG
7	JIM HARRISON
8	VAL FONTEYNE
9	ROSS PERKINS
10	RON ANDERSON
11	RON WALTERS
12	BILL HICKE
14	BRIAN CARLIN
15	DENNIS KASSIAN
16	ED JOYAL
17	RUSTY PATENAUDE
18	BOB McANEELEY
19	KEN BAIRD
20	STEVE CARLYLE
21	JIM BENZELOCK
27	DEREK HARKER

GENERAL MANAGER—W. D. 'Bill' Hu
COACH—Ray Kinasewich
ASSISTANT COACH—Glenn Hall
TRAINER—Ron Walters
ASSISTANT TRAINER—John Blackwell

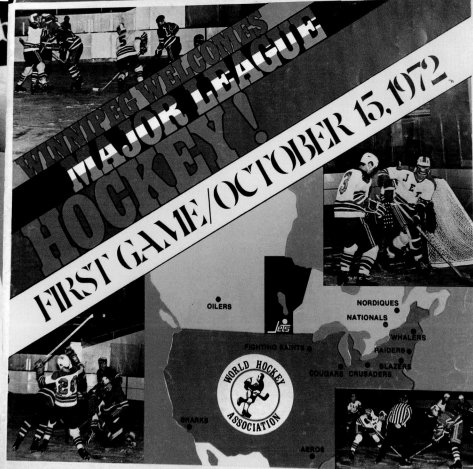

WINNIPEG WELCOMES

MAJOR LEAGUE HOCKEY!

FIRST GAME/OCTOBER 15, 1972

WORLD HOCKEY ASSOCIATION

OILERS
NORDIQUES
NATIONALS
WHALERS
FIGHTING SAINTS
RAIDERS
BLAZERS
COUGARS CRUSADERS
SHARKS
AEROS

ONE DOLLAR

CANCENTRAL CARD & SUPPLY

WINNIPEG

Jets
MAGAZINE

WINNIPEG JETS HOCKEY CLUB

SPORTS NEWS

WINNIPEG FREE PRESS   Pages 49 - 60

FRIDAY, OCTOBER 13, 1972

BORDELEAU FIRES FOUR GOALS
Jets Are A Hit On Broadway

By REYN DAVIS
Free Press Staff Writer

Bobby Hull couldn't play or coach the Winnipeg Jets last night, but he was still the centre-ice idol at Madison Square Garden at a pre-game presentation.

Reyn Davis

NEW YORK — "Hey, that's hard on the heart," said Bobby Hull, accepting congratulations in a crowded doorway where 25 writers were pawing for his attention.

"Not bad, eh? Not bad when you come out of the land of the enemy with two points."

Hull, the grounded playing-coach whose influence on this team has to be witnessed to be appreciated, watched the game from a ring-side seat behind the New York bench. But he could see the Jets quite clearly only a few feet over, where Nick Mickoski was pacing the bench.

You could see Hull cheering, but not excessively until the dying seconds of the game when New York, pressing for the 5-5 equalizer, appeared ready to pull their goaltender.

There was Hull standing up, shouting pieces of advice that wafted over the New York bench onto the ice where eager ears were listening. Seconds later, Norm Beaudin was terrorizing the Raiders' defence with one of the slickest pieces of forechecking this writer has ever seen. Goaltender Gary Kurt was unable to sneak to the bench under the relentless pressure of Beaudin, and by Bill Sutherland and Chris Bordeleau. Then it was too late. Bordeleau had scored.

"It's tough enough not to be playing and it's even tougher not to be allowed to stand behind the bench...

Chris (Pepe) Bordeleau, a little guy in a big town, made a lot of noise with his long stick Thursday night to send Winnipeg Jets off the tarmack in a blaze of glory.

Precision-quick and aided by two linemates, Bill (Sudsy) Sutherland and Norm Beaudin, ex-Black Hawk Bordeleau scored four goals, assisted on another and blew a breakaway as the Jets defeated New York Raiders 6-4 before approximately 6,300 fans witnessing the debut of the World Hockey Association in Gotham City.

With the Jets' trump card, Bobby Hull, watching from the seats and defenceman Bob Woytowich listening at home on radio, the silk-smooth Winnipeg club nibbled away until their first WHA victory was comfortably lodged in their stomachs.

Never were the Jets behind, but the Raiders twice reduced three-goal deficits to spreads of only one in what could be described as a tense, highly-entertaining struggle.

If the Jets had been overcome, the Raiders today might well be toasted as the great new hockey club. But they lost and sullen New Yorkers reserved blasting or boosting the Raiders until the weekend at least.

Tonight, the Jets skate onto Minnesota ice to be the guests of the St. Paul-based Fighting Saints, victors over Winnipeg in two pre-season games.

Then it's back to Winnipeg about noon Saturday for a good night's sleep, a peek at the kids, then back to the arena for the Jets' home opener Sunday night at 7:30.

Bordeleau's outstanding performance Thursday could hardly over-shadow the efforts of his own teammates.

The defence, reduced to only four men by Woytowich's inre...

closed the gap slightly in the second, reducing Winnipeg's lead to 4-3.

The Raiders still had a chance to tie the game and force sudden-death overtime when Bordeleau put the dreamers to bed with Winnipeg's final goal a second before the buzzer sounded.

Following the game, Bordeleau could not help but boast a bit about the Jets.

"They (the Raiders) were sloppy," said Bordeleau to a crowd of journalists. "These things happen, but I don't think that'll ever happen to us. We're much more disciplined."

Pepe might have been right at least this night. The Jets, all 18 of them on the ice, weaved pass patterns that would make a seamstress blush. It has to be that way this season. The Jets are too small to run over anybody, but they certainly seem to know how to go around them.

Ab McDonald, whose wife gave birth to their fifth child, a daughter, early Thursday morning, celebrated by scoring the Jets' first goal in WHA competition.

It was only fitting that the 36-year-old captain of the Jets should notch the goal. Danny Johnson dug the puck out of the net for the McDonalds' showcase at home.

Asmundson scored the other Winnipeg goal after Bordeleau outwrestled New York goalie Gary Kurt, who vacated his net to chase the puck in a corner.

"It was a freebie," explained Asmundson.

Ron Ward, playing centre and happy again after bolting Vancouver Canucks, scored two goals for New York. Bobby Sheehan, hair spilling down to his shoulders, scored the other two.

Sheehan, an American-born player, struck an instant rapport with New York fans who loved his explosive skating, hard shot and flamboyance. Sheehan appears to be the Raiders' first candidate for celebrity status in New York. Brian Cadle made only four or five appearances on the ice for the Jets, but his first, naturally, made some news.

His awkward style attracted New York defenceman Hal Willis who dealt Cadle a high stick. Cadle answered with one of his own, and Willis answered with another. Referee Bob Sloan, who happened to be watching, sent Willis off to serve two minors and Cadle one.

Willis was serving the second half of his four-minute sentence when McDonald, receiving a two-way pass from Johnson and Jean-Guy Gratton picked it out of the air for the game's first goal.

Bordeleau scored his goals, jamming the puck behind Kurt after Sutherland had fed him a pass through the crease, slapping a wobbly shot heading over the net that Kurt bobbled onto his goal; capping Beaudin's short pass from behind the net that Sutherland slipped behind his back to a wide open side, and, of course, winning the late, late faceoff to the left of the New York goal, then walking in to whip a wrist-shot along the ice between Kurt and the post.

All in all, it was a night to be remembered. The Jets will be back, but you can win the New York opening of a new league only once.

New York goalie Gary Kurt is tested at close range by Jets centre Danny Johnson

Summaries

Winnipeg 6, New York 4
First Period — 1. Winnipeg, McDonald (Gratton, Zarussi) 8:14; 2. Winnipeg, C. Bordeleau (Sutherland, Ash) 13:29; 3. Winnipeg, C. Bordeleau 2 (Beaudin) 16:55; 4. New York, Ward (Block, Bradley) 17:20. Penalties — Willi NY Double minor, 5:73, Cadle W 5:22, Cadle W 17:51. Second Period — 5. Winnipeg, Asmundson Bordeleau 14:34; 6. New York, Sheehan, Ward 2 Sheehan...

---

and Cadle took the first penalty — while drawing a double minor from Raiders defenceman Hal Willis. In fact, MacDonald's marker came on the ensuing Winnipeg power play.

The Jets had officially taken flight.

Three days later, the Jets hosted the Alberta Oilers in their first game at the Winnipeg Arena. An opening-night crowd of 8,000-plus took in the pre-game ceremony and player introductions. Both Hull and Hatskin received standing ovations. Winnipeg Mayor Steve Juba took the microphone and spat: "The National Hockey League turned deaf ears on this city for years. I hope they go into receivership."

Juba was mayor for 20 years. He knew how to work a crowd.

The Jets didn't, however, losing 5-2 to the Oilers.

An omen of things to come, perhaps. But enough about a skinny 12-year-old who was about to turn 13 in Brantford, Ont.

On Wednesday, Nov. 8, 1972, U.S. President Richard Nixon won his second term in a landslide. Next to the story of Nixon's triumph, on the front page of the *Winnipeg Free Press*, was the headline: "Hull Can Play." Philadelphia judge A. Leon Higginbotham, the African-American son of a maid and a factory worker, issued a 100-page ruling upholding the WHA's legal claim on players.

When the jubilant Jets left the ice, the organist played *This Land (Is Your Land)*.

The next morning, the screaming headline in the *Free Press* declared: "Jets Are A Hit On Broadway."

Ab MacDonald fired the first goal for the visiting Jets that night

As it turned out, Hull's administration would last longer than Nixon's.

The historic ruling came 15 games into the Jets' season, and just in time, according to Daley. "Believe me," the goaltender told reporters, "the guy (Hull) is so hyper about it, he's liable to murder the league when they turn him loose."

Alas, the 33-year-old Hull, after months of fretting, promoting and team-building — everything but playing hockey — had lost 10 pounds. Without taking a stride in anger, he was exhausted. What a hell of a time to quit drinking beer, Hull lamented.

It wasn't long, however, before the Luxury Line of Hull, Norm Beaudin and Bordeleau earned their moniker. The trio finished the season with over 100 points each. In Winnipeg, at least, the WHA was — as they say on the Prairies — a growing concern.

"You certainly didn't think you were King Tut, but we were starting something different, so you feel like a renegade in a way," Daley recalled. "Yet you felt like you were part of something that was going to be special.

"Starting out, when you went to places like New York, you didn't know if you were going to get five or 15,000. But we had Bobby, so we got crowds almost everywhere. So I didn't think I was in an inferior league or playing on an inferior team."

Indeed, Hull was drawing fans in Winnipeg and other hockey markets. The Colisée in Quebec sold out (10,126) for Hull's debut. The Oilers, playing in the 5,200-seat Klondike Place, filled the barn for the first time when the Jets came to town. Hull called ahead to ask the Oilers' flamboyant owner, "Wild" Bill Hunter, for tickets. Hunter sent the ducats to Hull's hotel, but made sure the courier collected. As Hunter harrumphed to *Sports Illustrated*, "We've paid him enough already."

But in Winnipeg, the Jets rarely sold out the arena, averaging less than 7,000 for Hull's first three games over five nights. Even so, the Jets were something of a mirage.

The WHA itself, from the start, was a dysfunctional family of wildly uneven franchises. A couple, such as Dayton and San Francisco, didn't live long enough to acquire nicknames. The Miami Screaming Eagles got a name but never played a game.

The Cherry Hill Arena in New Jersey, home to the New Jersey Knights — which didn't last a full season as the New York Golden Blades before relocating to New Jersey in 1973.

The New York Raiders were poster children for the WHA. They began as the Raiders that night hosting the Jets in Madison Square Garden, but lasted only one season before morphing into the New York Golden Blades, who didn't make Christmas the following season. Eventually, the team skulked off to Cherry Hill, N.J., reinvented as the New Jersey Knights.

Daley still remembers those hard Knights, too, in the Cherry Hill Arena, which — true story — had a sloped ice surface. The players' box was five players wide and three deep.

"The teams looked like choirs," *Free Press* writer Reyn Davis once observed.

TED FOREMAN COLLECTION

On some trips, there were more guitars than duffel bags. Singalongs on the bus

The dressing rooms were so small the visiting teams dressed in their hotel rooms... the Cherry Hill Arena — true story — had a sloped ice surface. The players' box was five players wide and three deep

'The teams looked like choirs'
— *Free Press* writer Reyn Davis

The WHA Winnipeg Jets,
1972-73.

Free Press sports
writer Reyn Davis.

The dressing rooms were so small, Daley said, the visiting teams dressed in their hotel rooms.

But in the relatively innocent days before thuggery became the calling card of professional hockey in the mid-to late-1970s, the Jets enjoyed the camaraderie of their collective cause. On some trips, there were more guitars than duffel bags. Singalongs on the bus.

Hull really had only one deal-breaker: No long hair. Brian Cadle went to the barber.

It was never the Cougars (Chicago) or the Sharks (Los Angeles) or the Fighting Saints (St. Paul) that sent fear through the Jets organization. It was the bankers.

Indeed, for all the ink spilled trumpeting Hull's seismic defection, for all the lawsuits and bluster — for the millions WHA owners spent to lure the game's stars and the millions NHL owners spent to keep them — the Benny Hatskins of the world never made a penny at the gate.

Later, Hatskin would confess to losing almost $500,000 in the first two years of the team's existence. (Even later, the losses would be revealed to be closer to $900,000).

"We went through some tough times," Daley said. "We never missed a paycheque, but there were some close calls in those early years. It wasn't a money-making proposition."

Consider that even before the Jets handed that oversized $1-million cardboard cheque to Hull, before a puck had dropped, Hatskin had seen the future. And it was expensive.

"The Winnipeg Arena can seat around 10,000 right now (slightly less), and that should be good for a couple of years," Hatskin said in May 1972. "After that, it will be a different story. Costs of operating a team are bound to increase, so what we'll need will be a larger arena to meet those costs — one seating at least 15,000. You can't continually keep raising the price of tickets. Fans will take that for so long, then they'll tell you to go to hell."

In fact, almost exactly one year to the day of the giddy celebration at Portage and Main, Hull attended a groundbreaking ceremony for a hockey rink in Kenosha, Wis., of all places,

and dropped a bombshell.

Asked about his new hockey home in Winnipeg, the Golden Jet bluntly replied: "It's a real nice city, but as far as supporting a professional team, they leave something to be desired."

Hatskin didn't run from the immediate fallout his superstar created. Besides, Benny was already trying to tamp down rumours that the Jets were for sale.

"Nobody in our organization is happy with the ticket situation here in Winnipeg," he conceded. "We're going to take another crack at Winnipeg this winter, that's for sure. But we're also going to take another look at things here. Everybody knows I want to remain in Winnipeg, but if we can't make a go of it, we'll be looking elsewhere, that's for sure."

In the WHA's inaugural season, the Jets had the third-highest gate (281,000), trailing the Quebec Nordiques and the New England Whalers, who dispatched Winnipeg in the Avco Cup final.

The Winnipeg Jets' Brian Cadle,
Elmwood born and bred,
photographed in Regina,
June 2011.

Yet despite Hull's tireless efforts and lavish media support, Jets season tickets were never a box-office smash. Corporate support, according to then ticket-sales manager Terry Hind, the renowned baseball player, was "terrible." The five major banks in the city held a combined 16 season tickets.

The provincial government purchased 550 season tickets to distribute to charities and community groups, even local prisons and halfway houses, at a cost of $100,000. In March 1973, three Headingley prisoners on day parole were fortunate enough to score tickets. They chose not to return. They were later captured and placed in solitary confinement to prevent "reprisals from other prisoners" when the warden suspended all future inmate ticket requests.

On the ice, meanwhile, the Jets couldn't get arrested. The club finished below .500 (34-39-5) and was swept in four straight by the Houston Aeros.

Hatskin and his silent partners, the Simkin brothers (Saul, Gerry and Abe), wanted out. By March 1974, the team was officially for sale and for the first time in the city's history, a plea that would be echoed for decades was first uttered: Save the Jets.

Hatskin agreed to sell the team for $2.3 million, with $500,000 down and the balance paid out over seven years, with interest, into public ownership. The city agreed to fork over a $300,000 loan. But the bulk of the funds came from, surprise, Mary and Joe Fan.

Between $25-dollar "membership fees" and $1,000 "founders loans," hockey fans and city residents responding to the Jets' siren call contributed more than $1 million of the purchase price — just as their children and grandchildren would do some 20 years hence.

It was the end of a short-lived era tinged with unbridled excitement, starry-eyed optimism and, ultimately, expectations never met. Of those original Jets aboard Northwest Orient Flight 215 to New York, only a handful remained after the team's disappointing sophomore season.

Cuddie left the Jets for the rival Toronto Toros after the first season and retired two years later. Garth Rizzuto was cut halfway through the 1973-74 season, Ernie Wakely was dealt to the San Diego Mariners (the fifth incarnation of the New York Raiders)

early in the 1974-75 campaign. Billy Sutherland retired and the Jets' first season was Wally Boyer's last.

And then there was Brian Cadle. By Christmas, Benny Hatskin's second-favourite player was a fixture on the end of the Jets bench, so much so that Cadle would sit on a folded blanket so his butt wouldn't go numb.

In all, Cadle played 56 games in a Jets uniform. But his ice time was probably just 100 minutes in total. He finished the 1972-73 season with four goals and four assists. Eventually, goaltender Daley would post a higher career scoring total (12 assists) in his seven seasons in the Winnipeg net.

But don't think for a second that Cadle wouldn't do it all over again in a heartbeat. Especially having the honour of calling Bobby Hull a teammate.

"Unbelievable," Cadle said of the other guy whose name Winnipeg fans chanted. "He treated everybody on the team — whether it was a guy like me who sat on the end of the bench — with the same respect, whether you were a star or not. He'd go on for hours signing autographs."

Cadle just couldn't keep up, however. "I ran out of energy," he said. "When you're 165 pounds and had legs like a chicken... I just burned out."

It didn't help, either, that Cadle was just as rambunctious off the ice as on. Too many late nights, too many parties. There wasn't enough of Cadle to go around.

After a brief stint with the minor-league Greensboro Generals in the fall of 1973, his hockey days were over. He tried university but ended up in sales. Today, the son of Elmwood lives in a trailer near the shore of Lake Pasqua, Sask., and is an electronic stereo sales representative. Every now and then, Cadle will remember the chants and rue the hard reality that the good times off the ice curtailed the good times on it.

"Regrets," he said, "I have a lot of those. But who doesn't, right?"

Fair enough. Do you think Hatskin never had any regrets about buying into the get-rich genesis of the World Hockey Association? "Everybody got rich," Benny lamented, years later, "but the owners."

WENDELL PHILLIPS WINNIPEG FREE PRESS

Corporate support was 'terrible.' The five major banks in the city held a combined 16 season tickets

— Terry Hind, Jets ticket sales manager

The Golden Jet, reacts
to play in Winnipeg
during a 1972 game.

And what of Hull, who after being estranged from the Chicago Blackhawks for almost 40 years, fell back into the franchise's bosom and confessed that he never should have left?

Yes, there were enough regrets to fill the old Winnipeg Arena. Just not enough spectators. And now the Jets were publicly owned, coming off the worst WHA franchise season the club would ever experience.

Hull wasn't getting any younger. The only mounting interest in the team was on their debts.

Only a miracle could save them. A gift from the hockey gods.

Then fate jumped over the boards, and took a shift.

In the fall of 1973, Dr. Gerry Wilson, the Winnipeg Jets' team physician, packed up his young family and moved to Stockholm for a year-long sabbatical to study at a renowned sports and health sciences institute in Sweden called Gymnastik och idrottshögskolan.

Wilson wasn't just a doctor; he was a former junior standout with the St. Boniface Canadiens who was destined for the big leagues. But Wilson's knees betrayed him. He had eight operations by the time he was 18 years old, cutting his NHL career with the fabled Habs to just three games during the 1956-57 season.

Wilson had been instructed by the Jets' head scout, Billy Robinson, before leaving on his Swedish sabbatical, to be alert for foreign talent, as overt bias toward European players had begun to wane somewhat after the seminal Summit Series in 1972.

On May 3, 1974, weeks after the Jets were put up for sale and a lost season ended, a small story appeared in the sports pages of the *Winnipeg Free Press*. It was the size of a coaster. Dateline, Stockholm: "Swedish Stars to Play For Jets."

Bobby Hull,
pictured in a
Jets program
in his No. 9 jersey.

CANCENTRAL CARD & SUPPLY

In a country where European players were openly mocked and the phrase "chicken Swedes" was a cherished insult in hockey circles, there was a distinct lack of fanfare for these two unknown recruits.

But, hey, desperate times, and all.

Anders Hedberg and Ulf Nilsson were their names. They were just 23 years old and they only knew one thing about Winnipeg: It's where Bobby Hull played.

Swedish Stars To Play For Jets

STOCKHOLM — Swedish international ice hockey forwards Anders Hedberg and Ulf Nilsson will turn professional and play for Winnipeg Jets of the World Hockey Association, according to a Swedish radio report Thursday.

The report said that both Nilsson and Hedberg flew to Canada to sign the contracts.

Hedberg, a 23-year-old left winger, was his team's best scorer at the World ice hockey championships in Helsinki three weeks ago. He was on the reserve list of Toronto Maple Leafs of the National Hockey League.

Nilsson, a 23-year-old centre, was on the reserve list of the Buffalo Sabres of the NHL.

"It looks like we'll sign a couple of Swedes for sure," said Jets' owner Ben Hatskin. "They must be top-calibre players because they held their own against the Russians.

"I haven't seen them yet, I certainly hope they will like Winnipeg and sign with the Jets."

JON THORDARSON WINNIPEG TRIBUNE/UOFM ARCHIVES

CHAPTER FOUR:

A Swedish Rhapsody

T HE young man from Stockholm looked out the plane window as it approached Winnipeg. It was May 1974. Anders Hedberg was getting his first look at the world beyond Europe. He'd never been to North America, much less to this foreign-looking region in the belly button of the vast continent.

Hedberg was travelling with Ulf Nilsson, his teammate from the Swedish national hockey team, on a great adventure into the unknown. They were flying in to sign up to play hockey in a league they'd never seen. But that wasn't the amazing part.

Anders Hedberg, No. 15, celebrates a goal in the playoffs during the Jets' second Avco Cup quest on May 20, 1978.

Gerry Wilson, who played for the Montreal Canadiens and later became the Winnipeg Jets' team doctor, with his son, Carey Wilson, who played 10 seasons in the NHL for the Calgary Flames, Hartford Whalers and New York Rangers as well as for Team Canada in the 1984 Olympics, and his grandson, Colin Wilson, who now plays for the Nashville Predators.

PHIL HOSSACK WINNIPEG FREE PRESS

Hedberg turned to Nilsson and whistled, *"Wow! Jag har aldrig sett något så platt!"*

"Wow! I've never seen anything so flat."

It was the horizon that Hedberg remembered so vividly. It seemed endless. And it was, really, for the young Swedes.

They weren't the first pioneers to arrive at the junction of the Red and Assiniboine rivers. They weren't even the first Swedish explorers to settle in the harsh climate of Canadian professional hockey, following in the wake of countrymen Thommie Bergman (Detroit Red Wings, 1972) and Börje Salming and Inge Hammarström (Toronto Maple Leafs, 1973).

Still, they were strangers. They spoke a different language, they played a different game. And they certainly weren't universally embraced — in particular by their new teammates, the Winnipeg Jets.

Yet together, along with those who would follow in their jet stream, Hedberg and Nilsson, both wide-eyed and 23, and the 30-year-old Lars-Erik Sjöberg — a high school teacher — would plant the seeds of a hockey awakening in North America.

Hedberg could have gone to Toronto, where the Leafs offered more money. Nilsson could have gone to Buffalo, the NHL team that owned his rights. And Sjöberg, the veteran, had been dismissed by the Minnesota North Stars, who considered the stocky defenceman too small to survive the NHL.

"We came to Winnipeg for two reasons," Hedberg said. "First, Dr. Gerry Wilson. And we thought it would be fun to go together. If it didn't work out, well, no big deal."

Wilson would often take his young sons, including 10-year-old Carey, to Elite League games. Carey eventually played 10 seasons in the NHL. The Nashville Predators drafted his son, Colin, seventh overall in 2008.

But in 1974, young Carey Wilson was just as enthralled by the Olympic-sized ice surface as Hedberg was by the endless prairie. "It looked," Carey Wilson recalled, "like they were playing on the Baltic Sea."

Clearly, the game was embedded in the Wilson clan's DNA. The good doctor knew talent and soon began paying special attention

KEN GIGLIOTTI WINNIPEG FREE PRESS

JON THORDARSON WINNIPEG TRIBUNE, U OF M ARCHIVES

JON THORDARSON WINNIPEG TRIBUNE, U OF M ARCHIVES

Lars-Erik Sjöberg, No. 4, skates past the Atlanta Flames' Guy Chouinard, No. 11, in a game in the 1979-80 season.

Anders Hedberg, No. 15, in action against the New England Whalers at the Winnipeg Arena on May 5, 1978.

The New England Whalers' Gordie Howe, No. 9, (left) and the Jets' Ulf Nilsson, No. 14, play in the Winnipeg Arena on May 20, 1978.

to his young intern, Hedberg, who the year before had played with the Swedish nationals in a four-game exhibition series against Phil Esposito & Co., then en route to their heroics in Moscow. Far from being awed by the rugged, star-studded Canucks, Hedberg concluded he was ready for the so-called elite of hockey. "If these are the best Canadian players," he reasoned, "no problem."

So let's all agree Hedberg didn't want for confidence. Neither did Sjöberg, who believed if Börje Salming could open the eyes of cranky, xenophobic Leafs owner Harold Ballard, so could he, Hedberg and Nilsson. If they came as three united, all the better.

In May 1974, Hedberg and Nilsson signed with the Jets for a modest $100,000 apiece. Said Hatskin: "I hope they like Winnipeg."

Without question, however, there was resistance. The cultural environment concerning European players in North America was draconian. The phrase "chicken Swede" was, indeed, part of the lexicon. Swedes were soft and couldn't take the physical punishment that permeated the game on this side of the Atlantic.

The prevailing prejudice against Swedish players in the early 1970s would make the Don Cherry of the 1980s sound like a one-worlder. For the Jets, trumpeting the Swedes' arrival, which in turn meant the inevitable departure of current teammates, wasn't exactly met with unconditional love in the Winnipeg locker-room.

"My initial reaction wasn't to throw my arms around them and embrace them like they were my long-lost buddies," goaltender Joe Daley confessed. "There was a little animosity."

JON THORDARSON WINNIPEG TRIBUNE, U OF M ARCHIVES

Mats Lindh, No. 19, wearing an apparatus to protect his broken jaw, plays against the Calgary Cowboys on May 21, 1976.

Hull and Jets captain Danny Johnson, for the record, welcomed the neophyte Swedes with bear hugs. But Hedberg recognized and understood the unspoken reservation some of his new teammates harboured. "What's the difference in today's society if somebody walks into a workplace in your office and they're from Sri Lanka?" he reasoned. "There would be some question marks to start with. And in the hockey world, an old friend was no longer able to be fed with a contract."

Yes, there was some resentment. Until Hedberg and Nilsson put on their skates. The reaction then was immediate — and electric.

Shortly after the Swedes landed on the flatland, they were on the ice at the St. James Civic Centre, practising with the University of Manitoba Bisons. Hull was already on the ice, tooling around with the puck in front of the net, when Hedberg and Nilsson arrived. The Bisons' head coach yelled out, "Bobby, go with the Swedes!"

Ulf Nilsson, No. 14, Anders Hedberg, No. 15, and Bobby Hull, No. 9, play the Phoenix Roadrunners at the Winnipeg Arena on Oct. 30, 1974.

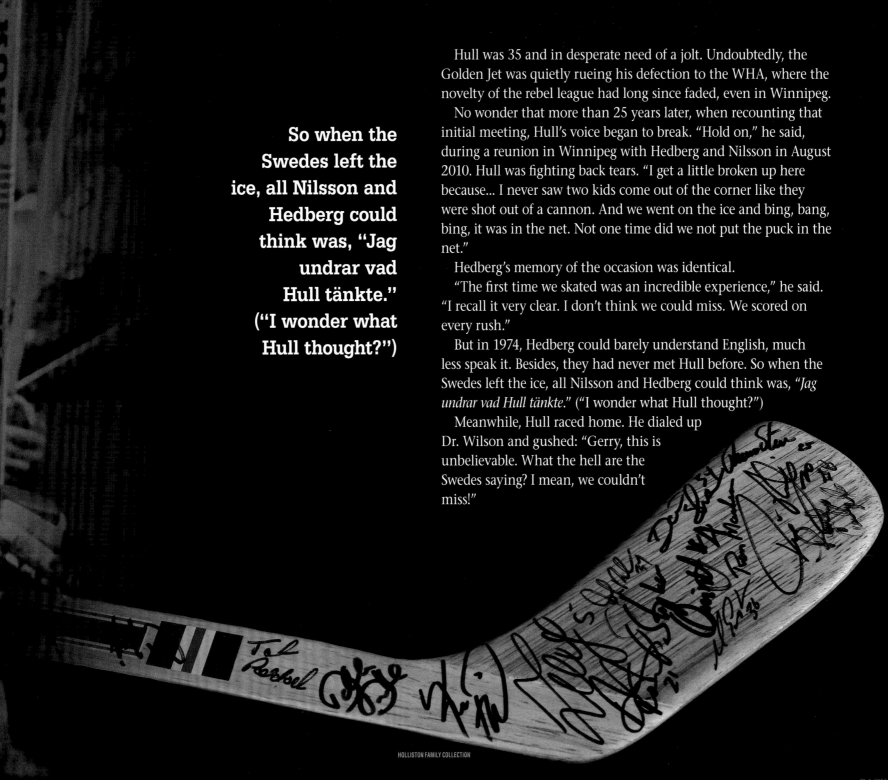

So when the Swedes left the ice, all Nilsson and Hedberg could think was, "Jag undrar vad Hull tänkte." ("I wonder what Hull thought?")

Hull was 35 and in desperate need of a jolt. Undoubtedly, the Golden Jet was quietly rueing his defection to the WHA, where the novelty of the rebel league had long since faded, even in Winnipeg.

No wonder that more than 25 years later, when recounting that initial meeting, Hull's voice began to break. "Hold on," he said, during a reunion in Winnipeg with Hedberg and Nilsson in August 2010. Hull was fighting back tears. "I get a little broken up here because... I never saw two kids come out of the corner like they were shot out of a cannon. And we went on the ice and bing, bang, bing, it was in the net. Not one time did we not put the puck in the net."

Hedberg's memory of the occasion was identical.

"The first time we skated was an incredible experience," he said. "I recall it very clear. I don't think we could miss. We scored on every rush."

But in 1974, Hedberg could barely understand English, much less speak it. Besides, they had never met Hull before. So when the Swedes left the ice, all Nilsson and Hedberg could think was, *"Jag undrar vad Hull tänkte."* ("I wonder what Hull thought?")

Meanwhile, Hull raced home. He dialed up Dr. Wilson and gushed: "Gerry, this is unbelievable. What the hell are the Swedes saying? I mean, we couldn't miss!"

HOLLISTON FAMILY COLLECTION

**Maurice Smith,
Winnipeg Free Press.**

The language differences didn't matter. Even Jets practices became events. Incoming head coach Rudy Pilous used to stand near the boards as the Hull-Hedberg-Nilsson line churned up and down the ice, their skates crunching with every stride. "Not only do they look fast," Pilous once marvelled, "they SOUND fast."

In their first season together with the Jets, the trio, which was dubbed the Hot Line, each broke the 100-point barrier. Hedberg was voted WHA Rookie of the Year. Hull scored 77 goals in 78 games, his career best. Nilsson amassed 120 points.

"These guys were the best I ever played with," Hull said. "God, it was fun. Even in practice."

Yet while Hedberg, Nilsson and Sjöberg are remembered as the Original Three of the 1974-75 season, the Jets also recruited Bergman, Swedish netminder Curt Larsson and Finnish forwards Veli-Pekka Ketola and Heikki Riihiranta.

To this day, Hedberg can't believe the team's 1974-75 edition failed to make the playoffs, finishing third in the Canadian division with a 38-35-5 record. But it was a defining moment for the franchise, nonetheless.

"Here's what was transforming about the Jets," said Winnipeg-based agent Don Baizley, who at the time represented Hedberg and Nilsson. "When they didn't make the playoffs, the consensus was (among management) that they had too many Europeans. They weren't tough enough. But Gerry Wilson disagreed. It didn't make any sense to him. He said, 'Why do we need fewer players we thought were good and more players who we didn't think were that good?' It was perverse."

Perverse, perhaps, but not unusual in an era when a Heikki Riihiranta might as well come with subtitles. Lamented *Free Press* sports columnist Maurice Smith: "To our way of thinking, it's rather tragic when a young man like Danny Spring — not the greatest hockey player in the world, mind you, but a prospect — will return to his home in Cranbrook with the thought in mind that if the Jets sign more Swedish players, his chances of staying with the team are nil."

**Nilsson, Hull
and Hedberg in 1978.**

**Captain
Lars-Erik Sjöberg
holds the trophy in
the Jets' first Avco
Cup victory parade,
May 5, 1976.**

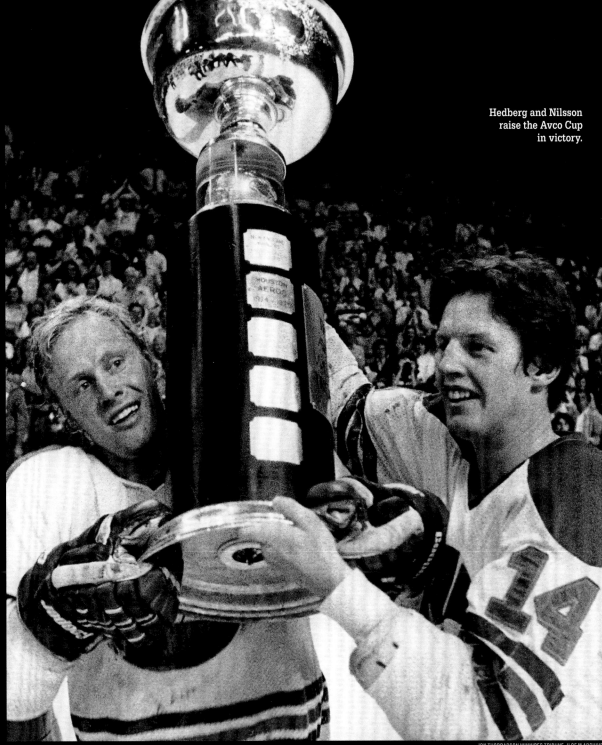

Hedberg and Nilsson
raise the Avco Cup
in victory.

Goalie Joe Daley (left) and Sjöberg flank the Avco Cup, the
second time the Jets won the championship, May 20, 1978.

Dan Spring didn't last with the Jets. Once a first-round pick of the Black Hawks in 1971, Spring was gone after the 1974-75 season.

But here's what was also transforming about the Jets: They won.

Instead of shrinking the European content, in the following year the Jets added Swedes Willy Lindström and Mats Lindh. In the spring of 1976, Winnipeg swept the Houston Aeros in four straight games to bring the city its first Avco Cup championship, destroying the Aeros 9-1 in Game 4. Indeed, the Jets won three of the next four WHA titles, losing only to the Quebec Nordiques in Game 7 of the 1977 finals.

That initial resistance from veterans such as Daley? Long gone.

"When you start playing the last game year after year, you're pretty thankful," the netminder allowed. "If you were fortunate enough to witness it, it was really special. And if you weren't lucky enough to see it, well, the stories are all true."

The Hot Line was arguably the greatest in hockey history, although the disparity between the WHA and the NHL makes any definitive conclusion impossible. The numbers are heady, though, as Hull, Hedberg and Nilsson averaged 143 goals as a unit over their four years together as Jets.

Said Vic Grant: "They changed the way hockey was played in North America. They redefined what a player had to do to play professional hockey. Their fitness, their skill and the way they played the game, we saw what happened when the Jets were in their heyday in the WHA. These guys ruled the league."

Hedberg and Nilsson, in particular, were truly pioneers who literally skated through a North American professional hockey gauntlet that future generations of Europeans did not.

Hull and the Avco Cup
in 1976 at Portage and Main.

WINNIPEG JETS VS. SOVIET ALL STARS
AT WINNIPEG ARENA
TUESDAY EVENING AT 8:00
DEC. 20
Reserved Seat $5.50
The management reserves the right to revoke license granted by this ticket by refunding purchase price. Holder assumes all risks incidental to participating in or watching activities. NO REFUNDS
CANCENTRAL CARD & SUPPLY

Joe Daley eyes the play as the Jets
play the Quebec Nordiques on Jan. 18, 1978.

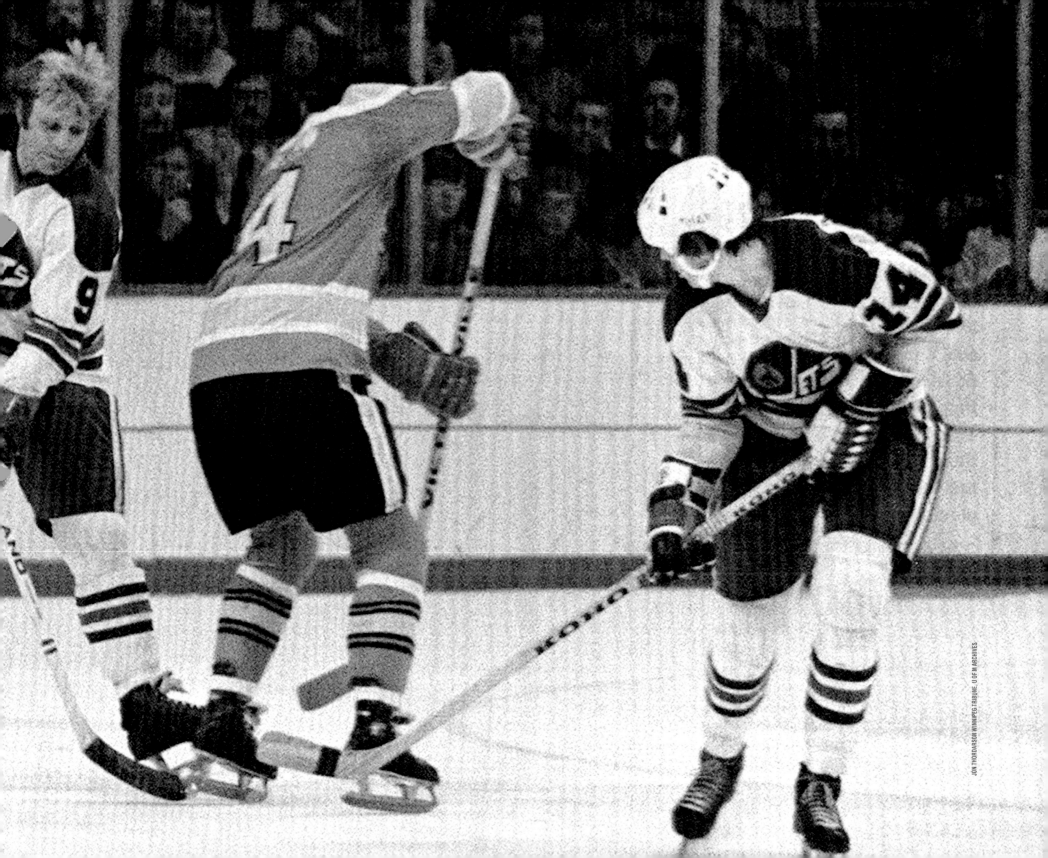

'They had people trying to run them out of rinks. Not anybody could have done what they did. They took the abuse and kept playing'

— agent Don Baizley

"Oh, it was tough," said Baizley, who has over the years represented a who's who of European talent, including Peter Forsberg and Teemu Selanne. "They had people trying to run them out of rinks. Not anybody could have done what they did. They took the abuse and kept playing."

It wasn't just competitive animosity. It was personal. It was ideological. And, on a physical level, it was often brutal.

When Hedberg and Nilsson, along with their Nordic teammates, joined the Jets in 1974, Barry Long was an old-school defenceman with the rival Edmonton Oilers. To Long, the Europeans were a scourge.

"It was a different era of thinking," he said. "Now we have this cuddly era of everybody loves everybody. Back in the day we didn't love everybody. It was Canada against the world, and that included the Swedes and the Finns.

"I was just as guilty as everyone else. I'd just as soon run them through the boards and get rid of them and send them back across the ocean. When I played in Edmonton, we tried to destroy the Jets. When I look back, I'm not proud of some of the things I did. A spear here and a whack there. And you could say things back then that you couldn't say now."

Two years later, Long was acquired by the Jets, but the likes of the *Slap Shot*-ian Birmingham Bulls and their ilk picked up where Long left off.

"Some of the beatings I saw them take to make a play... I saw some of the welts on those players from two-handed whacks or whatever," Long recalled. "They were black and blue. But they didn't complain. They knew it was coming and they just kept on going."

(Fun fact: At the 1981 world championships in Gothenburg, Sweden, Long played on a Canadian team coached by an irascible Don Cherry, no fan of the Tre kronor. Long patrolled the point for the Canadians and was swinging his stick like a lumberjack. One of the members of Team Sweden was a 20-year-old centreman named Thomas Steen, a Winnipeg draft pick who would go on to become the longest-serving Jets player in franchise history. "He (Long) is still famous in Sweden from that tournament," Steen chuckled,

30 years later. "I had people sending me letters to get Barry Long's autographs for Christmas gifts. They'd never seen a goon like that at the world championships." Ever-diligent Jets GM John Ferguson was in Gothenburg in April of 1981 and instructed Long — when shaking hands with the Swedes at the end of a game — to politely ask the young Jets draft pick if he'd be coming to Winnipeg in the fall. Spat an angry Steen, in broken English, "I don't think so, Lonck." However, just a few months later, on Michael Gobuty's boat anchored off the coast of Florida, Steen signed his first Jets contract for $100,000 a season and joined the team in the fall of 1981. But back to our story...)

On more than a few unruly nights in places such as Birmingham and Philadelphia, Hedberg would turn to Nilsson with a look as if to ask, "What the hell have we done?"

"Many times, it was like walking down a dark street, and you come to a corner and around the corner it's even darker," Hedberg recalled. "You have no idea (what's lurking in the shadows.)"

By far, Nilsson, who was a rakish 165 pounds, took the brunt of abuse. Hull was stronger. Hedberg was faster. On the night the Jets celebrated their first Avco Cup victory, Nilsson wasn't on the ice. He had been taken to hospital to be treated for a scratched retina. He took 12 stitches one night in a brawl with the Nordiques.

Nilsson was a wizard with the puck. As Carey Wilson noted, "He could dangle in a phone booth." For all his slight physique, Nilsson was one of the toughest hockey players Hull said he had ever seen.

"Players who went weeks without throwing a bodycheck would attempt to run him," *Free Press* beat writer Reyn Davis wrote of Nilsson.

The early beatings only strengthened the Swedes' resolve, however. Said Hedberg: "We became even more determined to survive."

But the toll on Nilsson was the most damaging. By the time Hedberg and Nilsson jumped to the NHL's New York Rangers for the 1978-79 season, the centreman's body was breaking down. Nilsson's days in New York were pockmarked by injuries: a broken ankle, a bad back, a broken arm and torn knee cartilage. He played just 170 games in three-plus seasons with the Rangers.

Nilsson took the brunt of the abuse aimed at the Swedes.

He amassed an impressive 169 points over that stretch, but at the end of the 1982-83 season, he was done. "I can't take it anymore," Nilsson said.

Yet as instrumental as the Swedish invasion was to hockey in general, the impact on the Jets' brand as a franchise would be immeasurable — even to this day. The indelible mark the WHA's Jets left is ingrained in the city's psyche. It became mythical.

The mystique of the Jets' mid-to-late-1970s greatness was magnified, not diminished, by their exclusion from the NHL. That's why the night of Jan. 5 1978, when the Jets defeated the Soviet national team 5-3 at the arena, became the stuff of legend.

Hull scored three that night. Nilsson added a pair. The Hot Line had 10 points.

It was the first time the powerful Soviets — led by the vaunted line of Valeri Kharlamov, Boris Mikhailov and Vladimir Petrov, along with netminder Vladislav Tretiak — ever lost to a club team.

But if you ask Hedberg if that was the best game the Jets ever played, he just laughs. "Oh, no," he says.

Rather, Hedberg longed for an opportunity, back then, to line up against the Canadiens' Jacques Lemaire, Steve Shutt and Guy Lafleur. Or he would watch *Hockey Night in Canada* and make a wish. "God, why can't we play Toronto? Quite honestly, I think we would have won many more games than we lost."

Not only did the WHA Jets pioneer European imports, they were ahead of their time in the export business, too. The Jets held training camps in Sweden and Finland. They played exhibition games in Prague. They represented Canada at the Izvestia tournament in Moscow in 1976. They played the Soviets in Tokyo, of all places.

They were the Royal Winnipeg Ballet on skates.

"I don't think that any team — prior to us or after us — did any more for that name and our city or the province than our WHA Jets, the way we travelled the world," Daley said. "I mean, I remember checking into our hotel in Moscow and the chambermaids couldn't speak a word of English, but all they could blurt out was 'Bubbly Hull!'; they knew Bobby Hull was in town and they knew the Winnipeg Jets were in town."

So here's a riddle: Why, all too often, did Winnipeggers not know the Jets were in town? Why was the 10,131-seat Winnipeg Arena rarely sold out?

You can call the WHA Jets a lot of things — rebellious, pioneering, exotic, exquisite or historic.

But there's one thing you can't call them: profitable.

All told, the owners of the 32 WHA teams lost an estimated $50

Soviet national team goalie Vladislav Tretiak at the opening ceremonies for a game the Soviets would never forget. In the first game on home ice in 1978, the Winnipeg Jets delivered a victory, final score 5-3, after losing a series of three exhibition games against the same Soviet team in Japan. The game marked the first time the Soviets were defeated by a club team.

million, while the 803 players who performed in the upstart league earned an estimated $120 million. Yet a season ticket for the 1974-75 season was just $214. During the 1975-76 season, single tickets to a Jets game ranged from $4 to $9.

It was a fact: The Jets were never an easy sell. If not for Hull, Hedberg and Nilsson, they probably wouldn't have sold at all. Not for long. It wasn't the NHL, remember, and the vast majority of WHA teams were motley collections of never-weres who were fodder for watered-down rosters populated by a dwindling number of mostly past-their-prime marquee stars. Worse, the games were rarely broadcast on television, which crippled attempts to market the league nationally.

Sure, the Jets were special, and they were without question superior, but they couldn't carry the league on Hull's broad shoulders forever.

Despite Hull, despite the Swedes, despite the championships, the Jets never made a dime. Hatskin claimed to have lost more than $400,000 over each of the first two seasons, then sold the team to a well-meaning public ownership group for $2.3 million in 1974. But not before the first "Save the Jets" fundraising rally was staged — a precursor to a tempestuous financial future — where 4,000 citizens donated $25 each.

In total, more than $1 million was raised from the public and business sector. There were again calls for a larger arena. Revenue could never match ever-rising player salaries. Sound familiar?

Hatskin's nephew, Ken Kronson, a Jets director in the mid-1970s, said the city itself was rarely able, or willing, to generate the revenue for even modest profits. The debt accumulated in buying the team in 1974 swallowed the cash flow whole.

"There's a lot more money around now," Kronson said in a recent interview. "An awful lot more than there was then. Things have changed. Maybe hockey wasn't as important. It didn't catch the fancy of people entirely."

By the end of the 1976-77 season, despite an increase in average attendance to about 8,000, the public ownership group was at its wallet's end. A last-ditch plea went out to local businessmen to take the reins of the struggling franchise.

During an emergency meeting at the Winnipeg Arena, a young entrepreneur named Michael Gobuty put up his hand.

"They were broke," he said. "They said they needed $500,000. But when we got into the books, we found out they needed $1 million."

Gobuty's family business was Victoria Leather, where, as a kid fresh out of Miles Macdonell Collegiate, he started out sweeping

Winnipeg Jets owner Michael Gobuty pictured in 1982.

floors and cleaning toilets. Gobuty, like Hatskin before him, was a bit of a gambler who also liked the horses. In fact, he owned Assiniboia Downs.

But when it came to running a hockey team, Gobuty admitted, "I didn't know shit from shinola." That didn't stop him from buying a majority share of the Jets in the spring of 1978, along with an ownership group that, among others, included brothers Barry and Marvin Shenkarow and Hull himself.

It was the unofficial end of an era. The WHA was a dead league skating. Only a handful of teams remained, and they were on life support.

At the end of the 1977-78 season, Hedberg and Nilsson could no longer resist the siren call of the NHL. Or the riches, for that matter.

In March, the Rangers offered the Swedes $600,000 each to sign for the 1978-79 season. The Jets had no means to match.

"When I saw the contract," Gobuty said, "I almost died."

Nilsson sounded embarrassed. "It's crazy," he said. "I've lost sight of what a dollar is."

Meanwhile, Hedberg realized the community that had adopted him could no longer afford the rocketing salaries NHL owners were, in no small part due to Hull's defection six years before, now willing to pay.

Long before Justice Alan MacInnes was appointed to the Manitoba Court of Appeal, he was a lawyer for the Jets who helped negotiate Hedberg's and Nilsson's contracts. MacInnes would become close friends with Hedberg and knew first-hand why he left for New York.

"Anders said to me, 'I love it here but I'm not so sure I want to stay and play because for me to play here, you have to pay me so much money,' " MacInnes recalled. "'I don't like the thought of Winnipeggers sitting in the stands and having to pay the price of tickets they'll have to pay to watch me. I don't think they can afford that.' That's why he was leaving. He had a real conscience. Of all of them, he was probably the most special. Very, very unique."

In a recent interview, Hedberg admitted: "If we had known about the merger, we might have stayed. But at the time, it was very uncertain. It left us no choice. We had to move."

The WHA was crumbling around the Jets. In the summer of 1978, the Houston Aeros folded, and the Jets absorbed the core players of their fallen rivals, including stars Terry Ruskowski, Morris Lukowich and Rich Preston.

In November, in a move rich with irony, the Jets hired John Ferguson — the man who had lured Hedberg and Nilsson to the Rangers — as their new general manager, replacing Rudy Pilous. But not before Gobuty approached Montreal Canadiens head coach Scotty Bowman with the job offer. "He (Bowman) looked at me like I was crazy," Gobuty reported. "He said, 'No,' but he was a gentleman."

Ferguson, in turn, hired a battle-hardened and hilarious head coach named Tom McVie.

Together, the collection of discarded parts won the last-ever Avco Cup championship on May 21, 1979, defeating the Edmonton Oilers, who employed a skinny teenager named Wayne Gretzky. On the night of the victory, a jubilant McVie was heard to exclaim, "This is better than sex!"

Yet even as the team's final WHA season was unfolding — with McVie's Jets finding their second wind on the ice — Gobuty was furiously working behind the scenes to persuade NHL owners to agree to a merger.

"We knew after we bought the Jets, the first meeting we had in Palm Springs for the WHA we said, 'It can't last'," Gobuty said. "Our only chance to be successful was to become an NHL team."

The NHL demanded a peek at the WHA's financial records and could barely hold back a spit-take. "They laughed at us," Gobuty confessed. "They looked at our books, and no one was making money."

Undaunted, Gobuty persisted, jetting around North America in a private plane with WHA president and Hartford Whalers owner Howard Baldwin looking for NHL allies, who included league commissioner John Zeigler and eventually even curmudgeonly Leafs owner Harold Ballard. Said Gobuty: "It took a lot of time and

BS, but that's how it happened in a nutshell."

Still, the NHL's board of governors, led by the Molson-owned Montreal Canadiens, rejected the first merger vote to accept the Jets, Quebec Nordiques, Whalers and Oilers, which triggered a nationwide boycott against the brewery. In Winnipeg, a gunshot was fired into the distillery's head office.

Lo and behold, the second NHL vote, held March 22, 1979, passed 14-3.

The Winnipeg Jets were in the National Hockey League.

Suddenly, Gobuty was a conquering hero.

"It was unbelievable," he said. "I couldn't walk down the street. People were driving me crazy. But — and I'm sure Mark (Chipman) will say the same thing down the road — it was a great awakening. It was a great time. It made me, shall I say, famous.

"We went from the so-called minor leagues to the best. In one fell swoop, Winnipeg was in the major leagues with Montreal, Toronto, New York, Boston. We were there. It was wonderful for the city. The Jets put Winnipeg on the map. I mean, who heard of Winnipeg before Benny Hatskin brought the Jets to Winnipeg? Nobody."

Yet if there is a moral to the Jets' rise from their WHA birth to NHL acceptance — with the myriad trials, triumphs and tribulations in between — perhaps it's that nothing lasts forever. Time passes. Fortunes come and go. Hockey players grow old.

By the early 1980s, the high-flying, fast-talking Gobuty had to declare bankruptcy. He'd lost the family business and the Downs. Gobuty's fellow owners fired him as Jets president and sold his share of the team for "next to nothing."

"I was only 40 years old and thought I could walk on water and pay everybody back," he said. "I did. It took me three years, but I settled with everybody. Nobody got hurt... except for Michael Gobuty.

"It (the merger deal) took a year of my life. It caused me a lot of problems. I took my eye off my business and put most of my time into doing the NHL deal."

At least that's Gobuty's story, which he tells three decades later from his home just outside Palm Springs. The man who once

'The Jets put Winnipeg on the map. I mean, who heard of Winnipeg before Benny Hatskin brought the Jets to Winnipeg? Nobody'

— Michael Gobuty

Joe Daley

famously turned down an offer to win the services of Wayne Gretzky over a game of backgammon with Indianapolis Pacers owner Nelson Skalbania in 1978 — "I couldn't, because I had partners to answer to" — has long since abandoned his former life as a jet-setting sports entrepreneur.

"I don't have that kind of money," he said.

But Gobuty wasn't forced to sell his memories. After opening with two losses on the road, the Winnipeg Jets played their first NHL home game on Oct. 14, 1979 against Don Cherry's Colorado Rockies in the newly renovated and expanded Winnipeg Arena, which now could seat 15,250.

The Jets won 4-2 before an announced crowd of 12,619, about 2,500 short of a sellout.

"I was so excited I almost wet my pants," Gobuty said. "To see all the work that I'd done, travelling all over the place from city to city begging people to get us in... next to marrying my wife and having my kids, it was the best day of my life."

The Golden Jet was never the same after his Swedish linemates fled to the NHL. Hull played just four games in the Jets' swan-song season in the WHA and only 18 more in Winnipeg's inaugural NHL campaign in 1979-80.

In February 1980, the 41-year-old Hull — one of the most gifted, powerful, entrancing players of his generation — was traded to the Hartford Whalers for future considerations. Hull dressed for just nine games in Hartford, scoring the final two of his 1,063 NHL goals.

Few might remember that in the fall of 1981, Hull attempted a comeback with the New York Rangers, with the hopes of reuniting with Hedberg and Nilsson on Broadway. But the magic, with their collective youth, was left behind long ago at the Winnipeg Arena, where you could hear how fast they could fly.

After five exhibition games,

Hull hung up his blades for good.

When the three aging Hot Liners were reunited in a Winnipeg hotel the summer of 2010, there was a touching scene prior to the press conference where Hull, at age 71, said to no one in particular, "Now it's time to get my shoes laced up."

So a man once known for his brute strength and blistering speed put a foot up on a stool and barked out, "Ulfie!"

Without hesitation, the 60-year-old Nilsson whisked over to tie the Golden Jet's shoes. Still with the teamwork.

"Knees or hips?" someone asked Hull.

"Knee," he replied, resigned, "and everything else." Hull paused for a second, thanking his old linemate, then uttered, "It's awful to get to 71. There was a time we thought we were infallible."

"Maybe I am getting more emotional," Hull said after the press conference had ended. "Because my life is getting more valuable now. I know that this isn't going to happen again (a Hot Line reunion in Winnipeg). I'm on the back nine and I don't have a lot of time. I'm not saying I'm ill. I'm just saying if I get another 10 years, I'll be luckier than a shithouse rat."

Hedberg talked about the "incredible feeling" of their glory years in Jets uniforms. "It just fit," he said. Did he ever feel that way again? Without hesitation, as if unleashing a one-timer in the slot, Hedberg replied: "Not even close."

Even on the flat Prairies, horizons end. Time still passes, even when old hockey players can't hit the tape anymore. When the Jets were finally accepted into the NHL, the only man to spend all seven WHA seasons in a Winnipeg uniform knew the final whistle had blown for him, too.

Joe Daley called it quits. The veteran netminder, at age 36, had a falling-out with GM Ferguson. Daley knew his game was slipping and had no desire to ride the pine as a backup. Not after what he'd seen at the Jets' peak in the WHA. And not before what Daley saw coming in the NHL.

"You can't go into the National Hockey League with everybody's 40th or 50th player and expect to compete," he said ominously. "That was the shame of it all."

Turns out the old goalie saw the last one coming after all.

'These guys were the best I ever played with. God, it was fun. Even in practice'

— Bobby Hull

Hedberg, Nilsson and Hull (left to right) at a Winnipeg Jets film première, reunion and Hall of Fame event, Aug. 18, 2010.

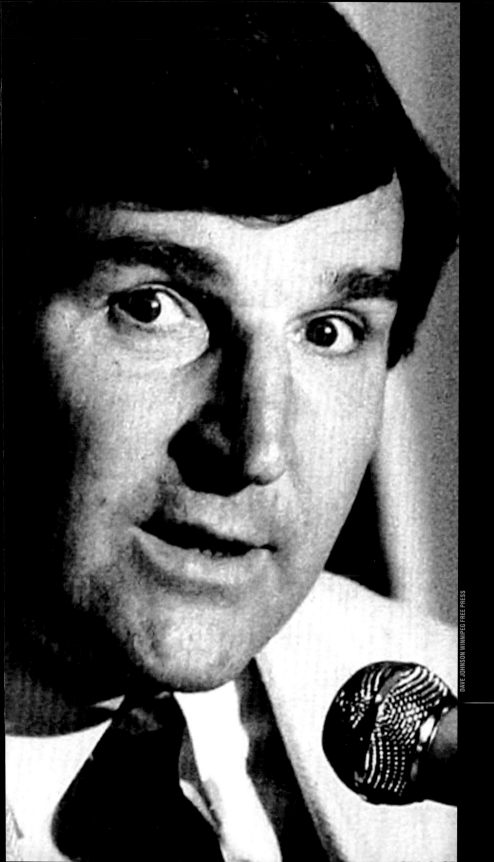

DAVE JOHNSON WINNIPEG FREE PRESS

CHAPTER FIVE:

Ferguson's Jets

I
T could be this simple, that hockey hated Tom McVie.

Perhaps, somehow in the past, or in another life, the diminutive scamp who escaped the mining smelters in Trail, B.C., had wronged the game's gods. Maybe it was somewhere along his 17-year minor-league odyssey that included stints with such wild west outfits as the Toledo Mercurys, Seattle Totems and Portland Buckaroos.

Jets general manager John Ferguson
announces May 17, 1985, that he has
turned down an offer from
the Vancouver Canucks.

Gobuty pursued a reluctant John Ferguson to be general manager because he thought Fergie's presence would give the Jets more credibility in the NHL.

Winnipeg Jets coach Tom McVie, pictured in 1979.

How else could one explain the utter lack of fortune for a head coach who managed to survive the travails of the 1975-76 Washington Capitals, a collection of post-expansion misfits coming off a soul-crushing 8-67-5 debut season? It was McVie's sorry predecessor with the Capitals, Jim Anderson, who once sighed, "I'd rather find out my wife was cheating on me than keep losing like this. At least I could tell my wife to cut it out."

The Caps lost 67 games. Then Anderson got canned.

McVie arrived in Washington midway through the excruciating 1975-76 season as the Caps were in the midst of losing 25 straight en route to an ignominious 11-59-10 campaign. Players were smoking in the team dressing room. One had gained 17 pounds since training camp.

Some nights were better than others. McVie recalls taking his poor Caps into the Montreal Forum. Before the opening faceoff, he cast a glance over the Canadiens' lineup card and muttered to himself, "Are you f--king kidding me? Not one of my players could make their roster."

Eventually, McVie would be put out of his misery in the U.S.

capital, where his punishment ended with his dismissal midway through the 1978-79 season. But that didn't make the gruff, gregarious coach any happier.

"I was five months without a job," McVie said, in a rich baritone voice that sounds like Rodney Dangerfield and Henry Kissinger had a baby. "It was making me crazy. I had nothing to do. I was standing on my doorstep yelling at the mailman. But Fergie saved me."

Well, sort of.

The Winnipeg Jets hired John Ferguson in November 1978, only four months after Ferguson, then the general manager of the Rangers, had spirited Anders Hedberg and Ulf Nilsson to New York.

The Rangers fired Ferguson in the summer — while he was in Winnipeg attending a farewell dinner for Hedberg and Nilsson, no less. Which is another thing: Ferguson was flabbergasted that Winnipeggers would actually hold a dinner for the Swedes who were leaving their team. For more money yet. "What are they, a couple of saints?" Fergie bellowed.

Yet even as Ferguson was luring the beloved Swedes out from

GM Rudy Pilous, pictured in 1974

under the Jets' noses, Winnipeg owner Michael Gobuty was openly courting the charismatic, ham-fisted former Canadiens enforcer, who was just as intimidating in a tailored suit. Gobuty wanted a place at the NHL table, and he believed Ferguson's pedigree with the Canadiens and Rangers would give the country-mouse Jets some needed *gravitas*. Gobuty constantly needled the tough guy about coming to Winnipeg to "freeze his ass off."

"When we started to try to get into the NHL, the merger, we needed some credibility, so we went after Fergie," Gobuty said. "I spoke to him once a week, and he would laugh and joke."

Both men shared a love of the ponies, so there was always something to talk about. When the Rangers unceremoniously dumped Ferguson, Gobuty pounced.

Ferguson succeeded Rudy Pilous in November and inherited a WHA Jets team, the final edition, that had been bolstered by the addition of former Houston Aeros stars Terry Ruskowski, Morris Lukowich, Scott Campbell and Rich Preston. The Swedes were gone, and Bobby Hull had announced his first retirement at almost the exact time Ferguson darkened the Jets' door.

Jets general manager John Ferguson speaks to the press in March 1986.

Gobuty (right) catches coach Tom McVie in a pensive mood at a 1979 practice.

PAUL DELESKE WINNIPEG FREE PRESS

McVie (left) and general manager John Ferguson watch the Colorado Rockies with a critical eye in 1980.

A jubilant McVie hugs player Kim Clackson as the team celebrates the Jets' third Avco Cup win in 1979.

McVie's plaid sports jacket was a victim of a champagne-soaked dressing-room celebration May 20, 1978, when the Jets won the Avco Cup for the second time.

Almost three-quarters of the way through the season, Ferguson concluded that the Jets, the defending Avco Cup champions, needed an adrenaline shot. That came in the human form of McVie, an unconventional fitness freak with boundless energy and a bottomless pit of enthusiasm. To this day, at age 76, McVie is quick to confess, "People think I'm on something. When my feet hit the floor, I'm running."

(Note: Now a scout for the Boston Bruins, McVie was interviewed for this book prior to Game 2 of the 2011 Stanley Cup final between Boston and Vancouver. Asked how long he wanted to remain in hockey, McVie said he had a wish: One day in the future he would file a game report for Bruins GM Peter Chiarelli, then drop dead on the spot. After a brief pause, McVie added: "Just not after Game 2." But we digress.)

So it looked as though McVie's listing ship had finally come in, what with the Jets finding their groove in a 1979 playoff run that ended with a championship victory over the Edmonton Oilers. Next thing you know, the once-downtrodden head coach of the sad-sack Washington Capitals was driving in an open convertible down Portage Avenue waving to the throngs of giddy Winnipeg Jets fans celebrating their third Avco Cup parade in four years.

"The whole city turned out," is how McVie remembers the occasion.

My, what heady days. The Jets were champions, again. They were destined, finally, for their rightful place in the venerable NHL. The big leagues, at last. And Tom McVie was along for the ride in an open convertible.

It was too good to be true — no, really, it was too good to be

Jets forward Morris Lukowich is upended by the Calgary Flames' Charlie Bourgeois at the Winnipeg Arena in the early 1980s.

The NHL might have charged the Jets a $5-million registration fee, but the newbies hadn't even begun to start paying the price of admission. In what might be the worst Welcome Wagon display in professional sports history, the merging WHA teams — Winnipeg, Edmonton, Quebec and Hartford — were allowed to protect just two roster players from a scavenger draft by existing NHL teams.

Reasoned St. Louis GM Emile "The Cat" Francis: "How can I justify it to our fans if I allow a new team into the league that's already better than we are?"

Ferguson chose to protect the offensively gifted Lukowich, who led the Jets with 65 goals in the last WHA season, and Campbell, a promising stay-at-home defenceman the GM believed had the makings of a young Larry Robinson.

The Jets were fleeced of 10 players, including their leading scorer, Swedish sniper Kent Nilsson, along with veterans Terry Ruskowski and Rich Preston.

Then it got worse. Chronic asthma, compounded by Winnipeg's bitterly cold winters, limited Campbell's brief tenure with the Jets to two seasons and 14 games, effectively ending his NHL career. With a decimated roster, Ferguson then used the Jets' first-ever NHL draft pick, 19th overall in the summer of 1979, to select a heavy-fisted forward from Montreal named Jimmy Mann, who in five seasons would score nine goals.

And so it was that the Winnipeg Jets took their first tentative steps into the National Hockey League.

Of course, McVie had seen this horror movie before, and he tried screaming in the theatre before the curtain rose on the 1979-80 season.

"Let me tell you a story," he began. "They had some kind of jamboree or something (in Winnipeg). We'd just won the (Avco Cup) championship. And the fans were chanting 'N-H-L, N-H-L!' I said, 'You've got to understand, they're going to take all our players.' And they said, 'We don't care! We don't care!' I said, 'You don't understand. The prices of tickets are probably going to triple. And they said, 'We don't care! We don't care!' And I said, 'It's going to be a long time before we can win games and get in the playoffs.' And they were still saying, 'We don't care! We don't care!'

"Well, after about five f--kin' games they were throwing stuff. They were pissed off. They sure cared after that."

It wasn't pretty. The Jets won just 20 games in their inaugural NHL campaign. Yet out of all the lopsided losses, there was born perhaps the most humorous anecdote in franchise history.

Or as Tommy McVie calls it, "the most amazing night in hockey."

The entire city was in a tizzy Dec. 15, 1979, when the Montreal Canadiens made their first visit to the Winnipeg Arena.

It was to be the first time a Jets contest would be broadcast coast to coast on *Hockey Night in Canada*. To mark the occasion, it was dubbed Tuxedo Night, and all the Jets staff were decked out in tuxedos, including McVie. And Ferguson. And the Zamboni driver.

The cherry on top, of course, was Bobby Hull, who had been talked out of retirement and back into a Jets jersey for the glitzy occasion. Hull was in the waning days of his career, beset by injuries, and would play just 18 games for the Jets his final season in Winnipeg. The days of Hedberg, Nilsson and the Golden Jet were a wistful memory, and early in the 1979-80 season, Hull was once paired on a line with Mann, the lumbering rookie. Scribbled the *Free Press's* Reyn Davis: "It was like watching Benny Goodman try to play cornet with the Bee Gees."

Still, one last fling was in order. For posterity's sake.

Turns out, however, since *HNIC* was airing the game, it started 30 minutes earlier than usual. The opening faceoff was 7 p.m.

Someone should have told Hull, who arrived late. So McVie, the no-nonsense bench boss, advised Hull that he couldn't dress. Those were the rules. No exceptions, not even for the Golden Jet.

"I couldn't pull a young kid out of the lineup who wanted to play the Montreal Canadiens all his life," McVie reasoned. "That's the only decision I could make."

Hull protested, but eventually stormed out a side door of the arena.

McVie knew full well what was going to happen next. Fergie was coming.

McVie and Ferguson were lifelong friends, having first met as teenagers in the rough-and-tumble East Side of Vancouver in the late 1950s. They were hockey brothers. As McVie noted, "It didn't

JON THORDARSON WINNIPEG TRIBUNE, U OF M ARCHIVES

The Golden Jet in the late 1970s.

Barry Long, No. 4, blocks Birmingham Bull Mark Napier, No. 9, in front of Jets netminder Daley in November 1977.

Long towels down on the bench after a shift in the final game of the 1978 WHA playoffs against the New England Whalers.

matter how much we disagreed, because John Ferguson loved me and I loved him. It's way deeper than friendship, way deeper than that."

But there was no love to be found at the old arena on Tuxedo Night 1979.

"So down he (Ferguson) comes into my office," McVie continued. "And he says to me casually, 'Where's Hull?'"

"He came in late," the head coach replied, matter-of-factly, "so I told him he couldn't play."

Ferguson was getting serious now. "Quit screwing around, Tommy. Where is he?"

McVie tried again. "I told you, he went out the side door."

Ferguson was getting red now, balling his big fists. "Do you know this game is going right across Canada?" the GM screamed.

"I don't give a f--k if it's going around the world," McVie protested. "He came in late. The team was going out on the ice."

Naturally, Ferguson, whose outbursts were the stuff of legend,

lost it completely, putting the first of what would be countless holes in walls or doors of the Winnipeg Arena with his foot.

"And he's jumping around yelling, and his face is, well, it was a scary thing," McVie said.

Before leaving McVie's office, Ferguson bellowed, "I'm going to ask you one more thing and then you're on your own."

"What is it?" McVie asked.

"Do you know he (Hull) is one of the f--king owners of this team?"

Demurred the coach: "Holy shit, I didn't know that!"

But the day was saved: The Jets with their humble lineup would prevail over the defending Stanley Cup champion Canadiens 6-2 that night. Outshoot them 48-18, in fact.

After the game, Ferguson was elated. Cigar in hand, he turned to McVie with a priceless grin. "When we were growing up," he told his coach, "I knew you had big balls. But I didn't think you brought them to the rink in a wheelbarrow."

Defenceman Dave Babych in Winnipeg
in the early 1980s.

KEN GIGLIOTTI WINNIPEG FREE PRESS

WAYNE GLOWACKI WINNIPEG FREE PRESS

McVie in 1980.

**McVie would
put a brave
face on for
the cameras
in post-game
interviews
then... 'he'd
go back to his
office and die'**

— John Ferguson

The Jets with their humble lineup would prevail over the defending Stanley Cup champion Canadiens 6-2 that night. Outshoot them 48-18, in fact

It might have been the last time that year Tom McVie, as head coach of the moribund Jets, would have reason to smile. In the team's sophomore year in the NHL, the Jets embarked on the worst season in franchise history. They won just nine games. From late fall of 1980 to the deep of winter in 1981 — two months and four days — those poor Jets went a record 30 consecutive games without a win.

Barry Long had been plucked from the Jets roster by the Detroit Red Wings in the WHA dispersal draft, only to return to Winnipeg for the unfortunate 1980-81 season.

"We tried so hard," the defenceman insisted. "And if we got a win, it was almost like the end of the playoffs. It was such a reward. We knew we were going to get beaten upon, but we didn't give an inch. People in Winnipeg were good. They knew what we were going through. It was tough, but it wasn't impossible."

McVie would put a brave face on for the cameras in post-game interviews then, in the words of Ferguson, "he'd go back to his office and die."

Long remembered nights when the head coach slept in his office at the arena. "It almost ruined him," Long said.

So Ferguson saved his childhood friend for the second time. He fired him, 25 games into the 30-game winless streak.

The previous summer, with second pick in the 1980 entry draft, the Jets had taken a mountainous defenceman named Dave Babych out of the Portland Winter Hawks. When Babych was first introduced to McVie and Ferguson at the Viscount Gort Hotel, he confessed he was nervous about making the 1980-81 team. "Don't worry, kid," McVie reassured Babych. "If you don't make it, we're all going to be f--king fired."

Babych was just thrilled to wear the Jets uniform, and on nights against the Montreal Canadiens during his rookie season, he would be in awe. "You're wondering, what am I doing here playing against these guys?" he said.

And maybe, as the losses mounted there were times Babych asked himself that same question, whoever the opposition was.

"You knew there were going to be growing pains, but... it was almost to the point where it was contagious," he recalled. "That's

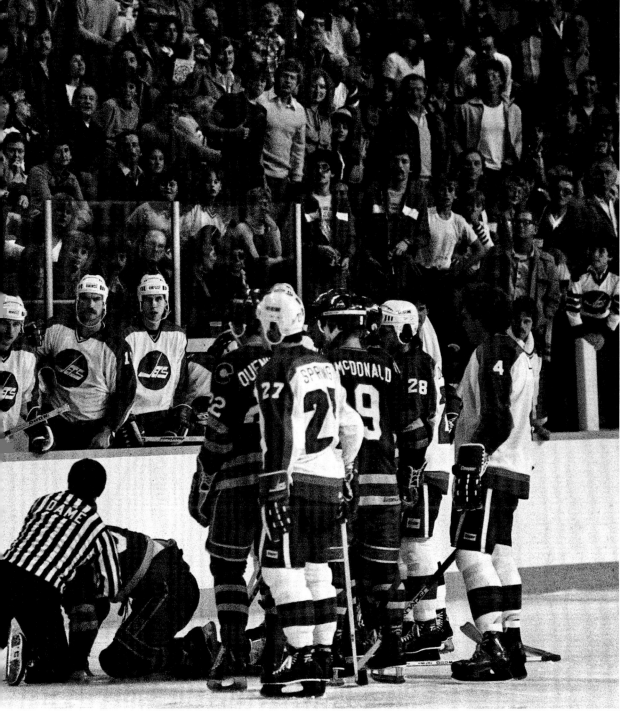

(From right) Dale Hawerchuk,
No. 10, Paul MacLean, No. 15,
and Moe Mantha Jr., No. 2,
celebrate a goal by Mantha.

Paul MacLean
(far left) after a fight
during a game against
the Calgary Flames in
October 1981.

Dale Hawerchuk, with Jets general manager John Ferguson, signs with the team on Aug. 13, 1981.

Serge Savard, Hockey Hall of Famer and one-time Montreal Canadien, played two seasons with the Jets, starting in 1980-81.

tough. Once it starts going that way, especially in pro sports, it can be hard to get it going the other way."

Without question, the hapless streak was the nadir of the Winnipeg Jets franchise. What kept them going?

According to Long, it was the trust that the suffering would not be in vain, that Ferguson, the organization's undisputed leader, would build the team up from ground zero. That's the confidence that Ferguson inspired throughout his decade at the Jets' helm.

"The first day he strode in there (November 1978) with that big nose and bigger mitts, there was that stare in his eyes like, 'We're here to win, boys,' " said Long. "The fire and desire to win, we all had it as players, but he demanded it as a general manager. And there were going to be no shortcuts."

Ferguson's commandments: Everything has to be first-class.

NEVER speak ill of the team in public. Community first. And don't trade draft picks.

"He (Ferguson) was very, very loyal," added Dave Ellett, a Jets defenceman (1984-91) during the team's most successful seasons. "He was a very intimidating person, and people were probably initially fearful of him. But when you got to know him, he was one of the best people I've ever come across.

"He was so loyal and protective of his employees, whether it was people upstairs or players. And when you got there (to Winnipeg), you could just feel that if you worked hard for Fergie, he would do anything in his power to protect you. I think, when I was there, that was the reason half our team lived in Winnipeg year-round. He created a real family atmosphere."

Ferguson began to build. After misfiring with Mann in the first round of the 1979 draft, the GM selected Team USA Olympian Dave Christian in the second round, Swedish centreman Thomas Steen in the fifth and American college defenceman Tim Watters in the sixth. In 1980, after getting Babych second overall, the Jets took defenceman Moe Mantha (second round) and speedy winger Brian Mullen (seventh round).

That was Fergie's way, a modern-day hybrid of his mentor, legendary Montreal Canadiens general manager Sam Pollock. "He was one of the first pioneers of using his late picks to find prospects in Europe and U.S. colleges," noted John Ferguson Jr., who was raised in Winnipeg, attending St. Paul's High School, before serving as GM of the Toronto Maple Leafs from 2003 to 2008.

Ferguson signed undrafted free agent Doug Smail out of the University of North Dakota in 1980. He traded for a plodding forward named Paul MacLean, a former Canadian Olympian, in the summer of 1981 — while at the same time plucking his old Habs teammate Serge Savard off the waiver wire.

In 1982, Ferguson used the Jets' 75th pick overall to grab the unheralded Dave Ellett out of Bowling Green State University, then signed undrafted netminder Brian Hayward, a product of Cornell, and traded for forward Lucien DeBlois, a future Jets captain.

Late in the 1983 season, Ferguson acquired former first-round pick Laurie Boschman, a centreman, from the Edmonton Oilers,

Hawerchuk takes a shot past the Calgary Flames' Jamie Macoun in playoff action in April 1987.

Hawerchuk, No. 10, draws double coverage from Buffalo Sabres players John Tucker, No. 7, and Bob Halkidis, No. 18, in Winnipeg in February 1988...

JEFF DE BOOY WINNIPEG FREE PRESS

...celebrates a goal...

KEN GIGLIOTTI WINNIPEG FREE PRESS

...and congratulates teammate Scott Arniel on a goal at the Winnipeg Arena in the early 1980s.

PHIL HOSSACK WINNIPEG FREE PRESS

then in an uncharacteristic move surrendered a first-round pick for wily Pittsburgh Penguins defenceman Randy Carlyle, who over the next decade would never play for another NHL team.

The defining moment of the franchise's early years, however, came at the 1981 draft, in the wake of that season from hell that almost killed Tom McVie. It was that hope for a better future that kept players such as Barry Long going through the dark forest of losses.

The Jets held the No. 1 pick, and Ferguson was being inundated with tempting trade offers. His choice was between a quick-fix trade and a prodigy from the Memorial Cup champion Cornwall Royals who was being touted as the next Wayne Gretzky. The kid was both shy and cocky. His game was both unorthodox and exquisite.

On the eve of the draft, held June 10, 1981 at the Montreal Forum, the Jets' brain trust met with the 18-year-old phenom, who looked big, bad John Ferguson straight in the eye.

"Pick me," said Dale Hawerchuk.

Dale Hawerchuk started skating at age two. Scored his first goal, playing against much older boys, at age four. Ask Hawerchuk, and he'll tell you exactly how he potted it, too.

By his final year at Cornwall, Hawerchuk topped out with 183 points. He was the Canadian Major Junior Player of the Year. The Memorial Cup MVP, Hawerchuk was ready for the NHL, even if it meant being drafted by a Jets outfit that had its own futon in the

WINNIPEG JETS MAGAZINE 1981-82 $2

FREE POSTER INSIDE

U OF M ARCHIVES

Edmonton Oiler Wayne Gretzky, No. 99, with Jets Brad Berry, No. 29 (right) and Dave Ellett, No. 2, in a game in October 1986.

NHL basement.

"Hundred per cent, I wanted to go there," Hawerchuk said. "I knew they had first pick, and I knew they were talking about trading it. They had a lot of good offers. (But) I embraced the challenge," he said. "That was my dream — to play in the National Hockey League.

"That's why I was never worried about a no-trade clause. In my mind, if they didn't want me, why would I want to hang around? And Winnipeg really wanted me. It was more of a gung-ho, hungry role at the start. Let's compete hard every shift and see what we get out of this."

Hawerchuk was the centrepiece of a Jets team that eventually began to challenge the NHL elite. In 1981-82 his first season in, the centreman amassed 103 points, the Jets' overall total improved a whopping 48 points, and the team made the playoffs for the first time. Hawerchuk was awarded the Calder Trophy as Rookie of the Year.

Laurie Boschman, No. 6, in a game at the Winnipeg Arena.

KEN GIGLIOTTI WINNIPEG FREE PRESS

"He had a calming effect. Dale's skating style... it wasn't like he was Igor Larionov or Mario Lemieux, where it was effortless," Babych said. "But when he had the puck, God, he could do just about anything. Everything was better."

In the 1984-85 season, arguably the most successful in franchise history, Hawerchuk exploded with 130 points. The Jets finished fourth overall in the league with 96 points — a franchise total that held until the Phoenix Coyotes eclipsed it in 2010-11.

Six Jets — Hawerchuk (53), MacLean (41), Boschman (32), Mullen (32), Smail (31) and Steen (30) — scored 30 or more goals. Scott Arniel and Perry Turnbull each scored 22. In net, Brian Hayward could stop an aspirin.

In April 1985, Barry Long, the old defenceman, was the Jets' reluctant head coach, having replaced the fired Tom Watt the previous season. And Long sensed a payoff for the lean years the Jets had endured during their infant NHL days.

"That was the year," Long said. "We were so good. The glint was in Hawerchuk's eye. He wanted to win it all."

The Jets opened the playoffs against the Calgary Flames, winning two straight in the best-of-five series. They could taste the Oilers, the defending Stanley Cup champions.

Then "it" happened. The precise moment, 14:49 of the second period, in Game 3, as Hawerchuk dipsy-doodled up the ice towards the Flames' blue line and jumped ever so slightly into the air. The Flames' grizzled defenceman Jamie Macoun rammed his stick into Hawerchuk's ribs. The Jets' meal ticket crumpled to the ice.

"They (the Flames) hit me a lot harder in that series," Hawerchuk recalled. "It was such a war. That one just caught me in a vulnerable spot, that's all."

If you listened closely enough, you could hear the cry of forlorn Jets fans along with the crack of Hawerchuk's rib.

From the bench, Long was crestfallen. "It was like an arrow through the heart," he said.

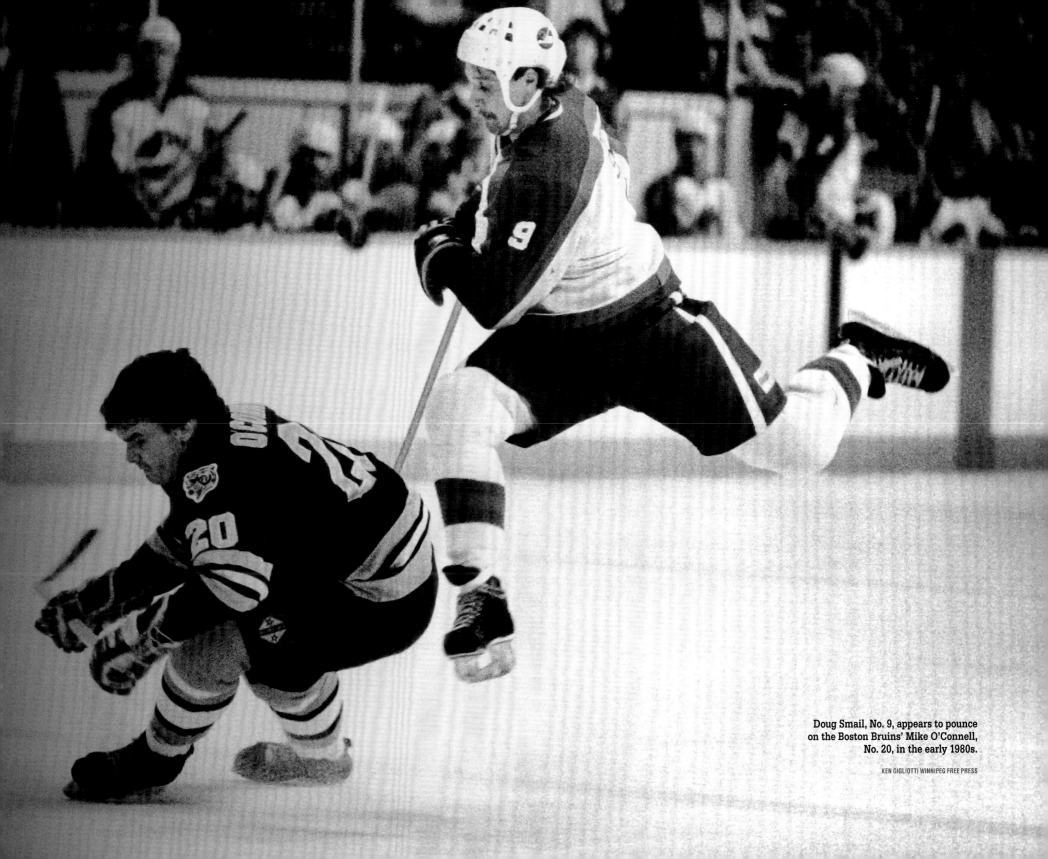

Doug Smail, No. 9, appears to pounce
on the Boston Bruins' Mike O'Connell,
No. 20, in the early 1980s.

An unhappy No. 10 unexpectedly turns his back on the team photo in April 1990. Later, he asked to be traded and left to join the Buffalo Sabres.

Dave Ellett,
No. 2, in 1989.

Hawerchuk was finished for the season. Even though the Jets managed to dispatch the Flames with a 3-1 series victory, they were no match for the splendid Oilers, who swept Winnipeg en route to their second consecutive Stanley Cup championship.

The Oilers dynasty, in fact, would in many ways define the Jets under Ferguson's regime. Good, but never quite good enough. Blame the Smythe Division if you want. If it wasn't the Oilers (1983, '84, '85, '87, '88, '90), it was the Flames (1986). If it wasn't the Flames, it was the Canucks (1992, 1993).

In fact, the Jets never did recapture the magic of spring 1985. Long was fired the following season and Ferguson traded Dave Babych for Ray Neufeld, widely considered the worst trade in franchise history. The Jets finished the 1985-86 season a dismal 26-47-7. *Out of Africa* won the Oscar for best picture. There was the Chornobyl nuclear disaster. It was that kind of year.

In the 1980s, the Jets had a revolving carousel of head coaches: McVie, Bill Sutherland, Watt, Long, Dan Maloney, Rick Bowness and Bob Murdoch. But only two playoff series victories.

In fact, what might be the most treasured playoff moment in the club's history — Dave Ellett's double-overtime winner against the Edmonton Oilers in Game 4 of the first round in the spring of 1990 — came in a series the Jets ultimately lost in seven games. Worse, they blew a 3-1 lead to a post-Gretzky team in the process — but not before assistant coach Alpo Suhenon questioned the Oilers' strategy after a 7-5 Jets upset in Game 1, saying the Edmonton players looked "confused" and "arrogant."

Oilers head coach John Muckler wasn't impressed. "I'm not going to argue with a genius," he said, sarcastically.

It was a careless slip of the tongue many Jets players rue to this day.

"That wasn't a good idea," noted Hawerchuk.

"We played a different team after that," lamented Thomas Steen. "We should have won anyway, but it was a lot tougher."

Question: Were the Winnipeg Jets of the '80s simply a victim of their time, at the Oilers' dynastic peak? Was their lot in hockey life limited by the restraints of a small-market budget as NHL salaries began to skyrocket? Or were they just not good enough?

Years later, Randy Carlyle believes the answer, like it or not, was the latter.

"We had a good team, and we had a good team for a number of years," Carlyle reasoned. "But so did Calgary and Edmonton. It just seemed we'd be up against that every time we got into the playoffs, and then Vancouver developed a pretty good team, too. In the West, you had to play at a high level and we never got to that higher level."

Asked why, Carlyle was his usual blunt self.

"I don't really think we had enough in our lineup to compete with those teams," he said. "The biggest area you can look at, and this isn't throwing any stones, the goaltending we had and the goaltending the Oilers had (Grant Fuhr/Bill Ranford) and the Vancouver Canucks had (Kirk McLean) and the Flames had (Mike Vernon), there was a stark contrast. That's a fact. You had all-star goaltending on those three teams."

Scott Arniel
in the early 1980s
at the Winnipeg Arena.

To My Good
Friend "Ted"
Jon Ferguson
1985

The Jets, meanwhile, never did find an anchor in net. Brian Hayward had a career season in 1984-85, but faltered in the playoffs. In 1990, the spotty play of sophomore starter Bob Essensa caused Bob Murdoch to blink and start rookie backup Stéphane Beauregard in the critical game 7. The Jets lost 4-1.

So were the odds simply stacked against the Jets all along?

"When you're living in the moment, you're not thinking of that," Hawerchuk said of the Oilers' formidable opposition. "You're trying to beat 'em. After you look back on your career you go, 'Wow, they had a pretty awesome hockey club.'

"I mean, we were a small-market team, and I was probably too young to realize it at the time," he added. "We didn't have a big budget, and we didn't spend. And back then, there wasn't a lot of (free agent) movement. I didn't realize it until later, when I went to Philadelphia. They thought they needed another defenceman, so they went out and got Paul Coffey. In Winnipeg, we relied on our draft and kids coming out of college. We didn't have the budget to go make that kind of deal."

Perhaps it was that small-market, little-engine backdrop that resulted in a level of bonding not necessarily evident on other NHL teams. Ferguson had his team barnstorming on softball tours in the off-season. There were golf tournaments to attend.

"He was a huge proponent of being in the community," said Ken Fenson, vice-president of the Jets' public relations staff in the early 1980s. "He was big in getting people involved. He knew the Jets were an important part of the fabric of the community, and he wanted to build on that. Because, let's face it, our first few years (in the NHL) were difficult on the ice."

Added Hawerchuk: "When you play in Winnipeg, you've got to have guys that care about more than just playing hockey. You've got to have guys that want to win for the city and the jersey and the Winnipeg Jets. That's what it's all about at the end of the day."

Jets board member Ted Foreman, right, with general manager John Ferguson in 1987 when the Sporting News named him Executive of the Year for the third time.

But in the end, closeness wasn't good enough.

The inability of the Jets to unshackle themselves from their post-season bonds ultimately cost the team's patriarch his job. Team owner Barry Shenkarow fired John Ferguson on an October night in 1988. The Jets organization was fundamentally altered when Ferguson was replaced by the man he had hired as an associate coach in 1980: Mike Smith.

"It was hard for everybody," said longtime Jets assistant coach and lifelong Ferguson friend and confidant Billy Sutherland. "He was the backbone of the whole team. Not only did it break his heart, but it broke a lot of hearts of the people involved with the Winnipeg Jets — management and players, too. I mean, when he was in Winnipeg, it was one big, happy family."

Added Ellett, bluntly: "That was one of the worst days in Winnipeg Jets history as far as I was concerned. They never should have got him out of Winnipeg. End of story. That was the start of the ticket out of Winnipeg.

"You saw what happened. They traded Dale Hawerchuk, a person who should have never left that franchise."

Oh, yes, Hawerchuk. Long before Smith was promoted to general manager, he had confided to Hawerchuk that if he, Smith, had been in charge back at the 1981 draft, he would have selected Bobby Carpenter instead.

Said Hawerchuk: "Mike Smith was never a Dale Hawerchuk fan. Mike was a negative guy. I never understood that. Once he took over, he was looking for a way to get me out of there. That's fine. I didn't want to hang around if that's what they wanted.

"I thought I'd play there forever. But it got to the point where it wasn't going to work anymore."

Smith dealt Hawerchuk to the Buffalo Sabres in June 1990 for defenceman Phil Housley and forwards Scott Arniel and Jeff Parker. The Jets also switched first-round picks with the Sabres, dropping

WINNIPEG FREE PRESS

Jets general manager Mike Smith in 1989.

from No. 14 to No. 19, and selected a big American forward named Keith Tkachuk out of Boston's Malden Catholic High School.

It was a good deal for the Jets on paper, no question. But it also marked a stark change in ideology where Smith's intellectual imprint, beholden to Russian and American influences, trumped Ferguson's sometimes flawed dedication to loyalty and gut instinct.

It didn't help that several Jets veterans believed Smith betrayed their old boss.

One day in 1991, Ellett was called into Smith's office. The GM, who stood casting a gaze out his window, never once looked at Ellett.

"We've traded you," Smith said.

"Where am I going?" the defenceman asked.

"Toronto," Smith replied tersely.

Said Ellett, as he left the GM's office: "Thanks for nothing."

BACK IN THE BIGS **99**

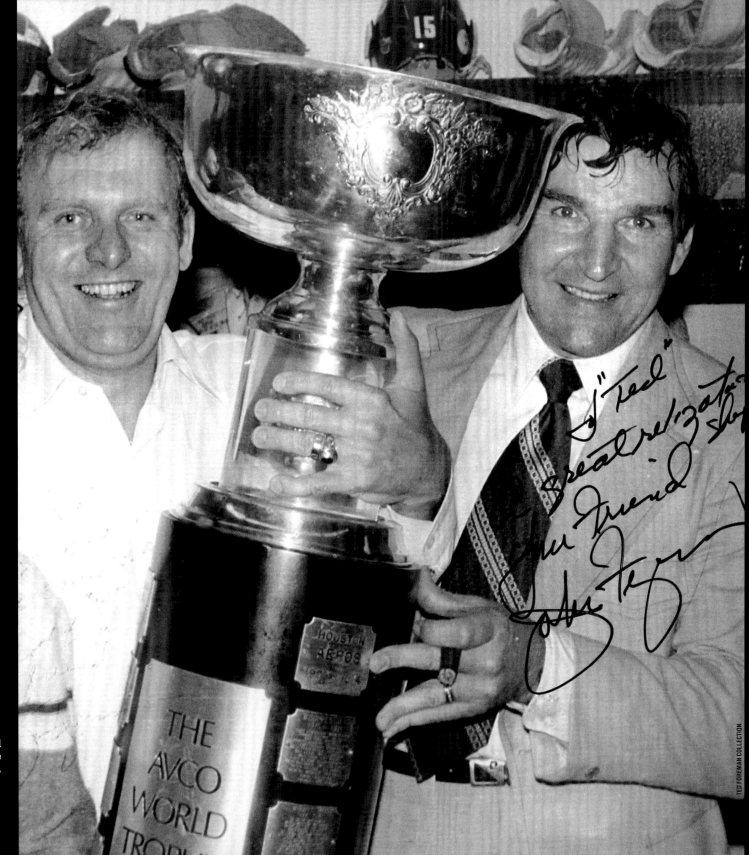

Foreman, and Ferguson hoist the Avco Cup in '79.

ON July 14, 2007, John Ferguson succumbed to prostate cancer at age 68.

Fergie was a gruff, friendly bear to the end. Ted Foreman was at Ferguson's deathbed, and the old enforcer grabbed him with one of those big mitts that once ruled the NHL.

"Would you do me one more favour?" Ferguson asked.

"Anything," Foreman replied.

"Would you do my eulogy?"

Foreman broke down.

"I absolutely lost it," he said. "But I got myself together and said, 'It would be an absolute honour, my friend.'"

It was one of the most heartbreaking, beautiful moments in Foreman's life.

"Now f--k off," Ferguson growled. "I'm going back to sleep."

After getting fired from the Jets, Ferguson served as a scout and consultant for the Ottawa Senators and San Jose Sharks.

"I'm convinced of this," insisted Jets communications director Ken Fenson. "He may be in the Hockey Hall of Fame in his Montreal Canadiens jersey. But I will bet anything — with all due respect to the San Jose Sharks and Ottawa Senators — he was accepted into the Pearly Gates wearing his Jets jersey. He loved that franchise. He bled Jets blue, and I wouldn't be surprised if he has a Jets logo tattooed on him somewhere."

Metaphorically, Ferguson's son, John Jr., knows exactly where that somewhere is.

"He had the Jets symbol tattooed on his ass," he said. "In many ways his loyalty in this day and age would almost be seen as a personal flaw. He identified himself most, by far and away on the management side, with the Winnipeg Jets. That never went away."

Before his death, Ferguson had one last fling with his closest friends, Long, Foreman, former Jets marketing guru Marc Cloutier, Savard and, of course, McVie.

They went to the racetrack with Ferguson, drank too much, and laughed.

And in the end, they said their goodbyes and left. But as they walked to the parking lot, Ferguson came running out and hugged them all one last time.

Bittersweet, you'd think. But not for McVie.

"It wasn't tough at all," he said matter-of-factly, at the time. "I've been 51 years in pro hockey and I'll remember those four or five days more than anything, winning the Avco Cup that last year, being in Winnipeg with all those great fans. But going back to see Fergie with my friends? That's the thing I'll remember most in my whole life in hockey.

"It was beautiful."

On June 15, 2011, four years after McVie said his last goodbye to the man who saved him, twice, the Boston Bruins defeated the Vancouver Canucks in Game 7 of the Stanley Cup final, and after 55 years in the game, McVie at last held the Holy Grail over his head. He kissed the Cup.

Hockey never hated Tom McVie.

It just made him wait, is all.

Ferguson, Ken Fenson, Jets communications director, and co-owner and president Michael Gobuty (from left) at the opening of training camp in 1979.

PHOTO SUPPLIED BY KEN FENSON

'I'm convinced of this... he may be in the Hockey Hall of Fame in his Montreal Canadiens jersey, but I will bet anything — with all due respect to the San Jose Sharks and Ottawa Senators — he was accepted into the pearly gates wearing his Jets jersey'

— Ken Fenson

KEN GIGLIOTTI WINNIPEG FREE PRESS

CHAPTER SIX:

Finnish Flash

PROFESSIONAL sports can be a nebulous, unpredictable world, a bit like *Let's Make a Deal*, where you never know what's behind Door No. 2 — a new car or a donkey wearing a hat.

Take the National Hockey League entry draft, for example, where the fate of franchises can turn on hasty, gut-instinct decisions involving the wet-cement potential of can't-shave-yet prospects. Sometimes it makes Lotto 6/49 look like a blue-chip investment.

Selanne was a
once-in-a-generation revelation.

Alexei Zhamnov, with the puck, in a game against the New York Rangers.

Exhibit A: At the 1988 NHL draft, the Winnipeg Jets owned the 10th overall selection and GM John Ferguson had his sights set on a speedy Finnish teenager named Teemu Selanne, who was widely regarded as genuine first-round material.

But the arch-nemesis Edmonton Oilers, who employed Selanne's hockey hero and countryman Jari Kurri, were smitten with the young Finn, too. The Oilers had an inkling of the Jets' interest in Selanne, so they attempted to jump the queue by prying the No. 9 pick from the St. Louis Blues.

In other words, the Oilers were itching to screw the Jets yet again, only this time on the draft floor.

A tentative deal between the Oilers and Blues was struck, but with one caveat: If highly touted Michigan State prospect Rod Brind'Amour was still available at No. 9, the Blues were going to grab him. The deal with the Oilers would be off.

To the Jets' good fortune, Brind'Amour was still available at No. 9 and Fergie had his man (not Mann) in Selanne. For once, the Jets beat the Oilers, who with the 19th pick selected François Leroux, a burly defenceman who would score three goals in 249 NHL games.

(Such serendipity works both ways. In 1991, the Jets drafted fourth overall and took defenceman Aaron Ward. With the next pick, the Philadelphia Flyers selected Peter Forsberg. Imagine, Jets fans, a decade of Forsberg and Selanne on the same line in Winnipeg. And if that tantalizing scenario had occurred, would it have led to a Stanley Cup? Would the team have left? Discuss.)

Still, Selanne was an unproven commodity, who, prior to being drafted, had played junior hockey in Finland, not exactly the hostile proving ground of Moose Jaw or Peterborough. But the kid wasn't an unknown, either.

Winnipeg agent Don Baizley, who cut his teeth representing the likes of Anders Hedberg and Ulf Nilsson, had a client list that included some of the finest young players in the game: Joe Sakic, Theo Fleury, Forsberg, Paul Kariya and Saku Koivu. Baizley was considered the global expert on Finnish talent, dating back to his association with early WHA Jets such as Veli-Pekka Ketola and Heikki Riihiranta.

Baizley relied heavily on his network of bird dogs who scoured the Nordic countries, and few were more reliable than Lawrence "Marshall" Johnston, a proud son of Birch Hills, Sask., who once toiled in white skates for the California Golden Seals in the early 1970s. "Players just don't wear white skates," Johnston once lamented, "and this one loudmouth hollered, 'Hey, Johnston, where's your purse?'" — this was before he rose to the position of Ottawa Senators GM in the late 1990s.

But in 1988, Johnston was a Prairie-hardened scout who had followed young Selanne's junior career in Jokerit. Baizley, meanwhile, grew up playing junior hockey with the Winnipeg Rangers as, in his own words, "a fourth-liner on a three-line team." As a hockey player, Baizley made a great lawyer, and generations of Jets players, in particular, would be grateful.

Baizley had competition for Selanne, however, and prior to getting on a plane to Helsinki to woo the young man as a client, the agent double-checked the kid's bona fides with Johnston.

"Let me be clear," Baizley told Johnston over the phone. "So you're telling me that barring some sort of unforeseen traumatic event or tragic accident, this guy is going to be an elite NHL player for a long time?"

There was a pause on the other end of the line and Baizley could almost see Johnston toying with a toothpick in his mouth.

"Well," the scout allowed finally, "it would have to be a pretty bad accident."

Baizley was sold, and soon Selanne was part of his formidable stable of clients and the property of the Winnipeg Jets. It would be four years, however, before a 22-year-old Selanne finally deemed himself ready for the NHL — by which time Ferguson had long since been replaced by his successor, Mike Smith, and Selanne had become a restricted free agent.

Smith didn't want to pay Selanne a cent over $400,000 a season, which was the salary the Jets had agreed to pay slick Russian rookie Alexei Zhamnov. Baizley respectfully disagreed and proceeded to shop his Finnish client around to all other NHL teams. There were no takers.

Baizley persisted, and finally the Calgary Flames offered Selanne a deal that was about $1 million richer. Smith called the Flames' offer "ridiculous," yet the Jets reluctantly matched, signing the young Finn for $2.7 million over three years. But Smith was not shy about his displeasure.

"I'm going to be shopping him around for the next few days," the Winnipeg GM sniffed. "The offers I get will determine whether or not we keep him."

And that's how Teemu Selanne became the world's highest-paid kindergarten teacher, having spent the previous three years instructing tots in Finland as the clock to his free agent status counted down.

Keith Tkachuk, No. 7, crosses the blue line for a slapshot in this game against the Pittsburgh Penguins in January 1992.

Squeezing the extra coin out of a cash-strapped organization didn't exactly endear Selanne to either management or fans. Indeed, the first reviews when the young Finn finally arrived for training camp in September 1992 were stoically noncommittal at best.

"His speed will always create opportunities for himself and the team he's playing with," offered Jets head coach John Paddock in the early days of scrimmages. "Other than that, it's probably an adjustment for him, in that he's just another player now. That's probably how he wants it to be, but he's used to being a star to the people over there. He's certainly a potential star here, but really, especially in training camp, he's just another player and he hasn't done anything to show he's not just another player."

Fair enough.

What happened next, of course, even old bird dog Marshall Johnston could not have predicted.

Selanne was a once-in-a-generation revelation. Good thing, too, because the Winnipeg Jets needed a saviour. After all, former franchise player Dale Hawerchuk was ensconced in Buffalo following his less-than-cordial parting. In return for Hawerchuk, Smith had acquired one of the league's most gifted offensive defencemen in Phil Housley, along with a first-round pick the Jets used to select bruising American forward Keith Tkachuk, who had game and a classic working-class Boston demeanour.

In other words, Tkachuk was wicked good — a classic power forward in the mould of a young Cam Neely.

Zhamnov, meanwhile, was a tantalizing enigma who had the confounding ability to score five goals in one game — April 1, 1995 — then disappear for the next five. But along with the veteran Jet lifer Steen and promising young defencemen in Teppo Numminen and Fredrik Olausson, the Jets at last possessed a commodity not seen in the franchise since the mid-1980s: hope.

Undoubtedly, however, it was the unforeseen magic of Selanne's rookie season that would endure. The kindergarten teacher arrived in Winnipeg with a humble, smiling exterior that hid a steely "I'll-show-you" determination.

Teemu Selanne, No. 8, in a game against the Dallas Stars.

JOE BRYKSA WINNIPEG FREE PRESS

Tkachuk tries to put it past St. Louis Blues netminder Bruce Racine.

But even Selanne couldn't have envisioned one of the greatest debut campaigns in NHL history. He fired 24 goals in his first 29 games, playing on a line with Tkachuk and Zhamnov. The trio was dubbed the Olympic Line, as all three had represented their respective countries at the 1992 Winter Games in Albertville, France.

It was the birth of Teemu-mania.

"There's great players, and there's great players with a flair," Paddock explained, in a lengthy interview in the summer of 2011. "His personality and exuberance and excitement to play the game... it certainly caught on with everybody in the city and the province. Hawerchuk was a great player, Tkachuk was a great player, but neither of them had that personality that people just swarmed to.

"There'd been nothing like that for the team after or before, especially during his rookie season," Paddock added. "We were big news wherever we went. Big news."

JOE BRYKSA WINNIPEG FREE PRESS

Selanne with Eddie Belfour
in the Chicago Blackhawks' net.

Selanne in a game against the Calgary Flames
during his record-breaking rookie season.

Selanne was a marketer's dream — handsome, self-effacing, just as quick to smile as shoot. Wrote Johnette Howard of *Sports Illustrated*: "If Selanne's wit doesn't charm someone first, his unebbing enthusiasm, his slack-jawed smile or wide-eyed look of wonder probably will."

Meanwhile, Selanne kept pouring pucks into opponents' nets at a pace that left even his fellow Jets in awe.

"How somebody can do that in his rookie year is amazing," marvelled Jets assistant coach Alpo Suhonen, a fellow Finn. "I'm surprised. Isn't everyone surprised?"

As Selanne's fame grew in North America, he was becoming an icon back home in Finland. For the first time in NHL history, a game during his rookie season between the Kings and Jets was broadcast live in Finland, the marquee performers being Selanne and L.A.'s Jari Kurri.

Suhonen estimated the Finnish audience to have been in the range of one million. "They've never seen Kurri, Gretzky, Teemu play live in the NHL," he said at the time. "They've seen them play on tape, like the next day, and they've seen them play in Finland, but never like this before. What's special is Teemu. Finns want to see for sure: After he has set these records, how does he look now?"

Good enough, apparently. When Finland junior national team coach and Jets scout Timo Sutinen landed in Winnipeg for a visit, he offered Selanne some free advice.

"I told Teemu not to go back to Finland," he said. "I see even here (in Winnipeg) he is torn to go everywhere. At home, every magazine you open, you see his face."

Sutinen noted that Kurri, already a household name in Finland, had a hockey school near Helsinki that Selanne had attended as a guest instructor the previous three years. "I'm afraid poor Jari might be lonely," Sutinen said. "All the fans will be asking him, 'Where's Teemu?' He's going to have to come to Winnipeg if he wants any rest."

The media focus was unprecedented for the little old Jets. Road trips to other Canadian cities resembled scenes from *A Hard Day's Night*, with fans trailing the Jets' bus in taxicabs or on foot and cornering Selanne for autographs.

"I mean, this is just Winnipeg," explained Jets media communications officer Mike O'Hearn. "Nothing really happens like this around here. It's like escorting a rock star."

John Paddock was of hardy Manitoba stock, a farm boy from Oak River who, as a rangy forward, managed to play almost 80 NHL games with the Flyers, Nordiques and Capitals, although the bulk of his career was spent toiling in the minors. He speaks softly and chooses his words carefully. As such, the head coach of the Jets in 1991 has never been accused of being overly effusive.

Yet even the stoic coach remembered a night in Calgary when Flames fans arrived early just to catch a glimpse of the Winnipeg phenom at the pre-game skate. Paddock rarely watched warm-ups, but that night, for no particular reason, he wanted to get a sense of the electricity Selanne was generating.

The Flames fans had lined up around the glass in the Jets' end of the arena. When Selanne bolted out on the ice (always right after the team's goalies), Paddock's curiosity was answered.

"You could hear a murmur going through the crowd," he recalled. "It was like, 'There he is!' It was something you had to be there to feel. It felt like being in the Montreal Forum and the buzz when Guy Lafleur came on the ice. And that was from the visiting crowd in Calgary."

Selanne's torrid pace was expected to abate, of course. He was a rookie, after all, and such streaks simply can't last the entire season, right? Yet by mid-January, despite a Christmas "slump," Selanne had reached the 35-goal mark — and suddenly the NHL rookie goal-scoring record of 53, set by New York Islanders Hall of Famer Mike Bossy in 1977-78, was a distinct possibility.

"I know I'm getting closer but I don't want to think about it," Selanne said. "It's not good for me. It's better not to think about it."

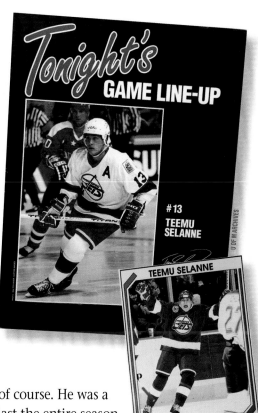

Lightning goaltender Wendell Young best described the helpless feeling of an unfettered Selanne driving towards the net alone. 'You just bend over,' Young shrugged, 'and kiss your butt goodbye'

Not thinking worked. Selanne was unstoppable. Two or three times each game, or so it seemed, Housley would find a streaking Selanne with a stretch pass that would send the Finnish Flash on a clear-cut breakaway.

"I remember every goal that year," Selanne said years later. "I remember getting, like, two, three breakaways every game. Nowadays, you get three, four the whole season."

Pretty good, yes. Selanne's goal total kept rising like the burgers-served sign outside a McDonald's. He was relentless. Selanne fired a hat trick on Feb. 28, 1993 in a 7-6 victory over the Minnesota North Stars at the Winnipeg Arena. The second of the goals was his magic 50th.

A few nights later, with the Quebec Nordiques in town, Selanne's signature moment came late in the game, with a late goal — his third of the night — that eclipsed Bossy's record. After depositing the historic marker, Selanne tossed one glove high into the air and took aim using his stick as an imaginary rifle.

Even opponents were left star-struck. Selanne scored his 57th, 58th and 59th in Tampa Bay a few nights later — the final tally coming on a penalty shot — and afterwards the Lightning trainer came to his Jets counterpart asking for three Selanne-autographed pucks. When told that would be no problem, the Tampa trainer replied, "Good. Then we'd like 10 more."

Perhaps Lightning goaltender Wendell Young best described the helpless feeling of an unfettered Selanne driving towards the net alone. "You just bend over," Young shrugged, "and kiss your butt goodbye."

Amid the frenzy, however, it was Selanne himself who offered a rather innocent statement that, in retrospect, became somewhat prophetic. Even ominous.

"Every time you set a league record, there is something of significance that goes along with it," he said. "I think it's great. It brings attention to the team and it brings attention to the city. Now I just hope the city and the team take advantage of it."

Winnipeg Free Press
Sunday

956-7270

Scott Taylor

Winnipeg Free Press

Sports

Wednesday, March 3, 1993

Editor, Julian Rachey / 697-7300

SECTION **D**1

Teemu gets it done!

But Jets let Quebec get away

HOCKEY

By Tim Campbell
Sports Writer

THERE WAS no chipping and nibbling away at this record. Teemu Selanne put it in his sights and simply blew it out of the water, just like he shot...glove last night...goal of...

...HOUSE

Jets' super rookie Teemu Selanne got his team on the board in the first minute of the game and it was a time to celebrate.

PHIL HOSSACK/WINNIPEG FREE PRESS

...citation, for celebration and pletely and surrendered four goals in 3:34 to lose 7-4 to the Nords.
"That's quite a way to break the record, seven goals in the last two games, and it didn't allow any pressure to build," said Jets' assistant coach Terry Simpson, subbing last night for John Paddock, who was at home with the flu.
"But we...

Pats on back

After depositing the historic marker, Selanne tossed one glove high into the air and took aim using his stick as an imaginary rifle

Teemu Selanne autographed game-worn gloves

BACK IN THE BIGS **113**

'We are headed for a crisis, and I believe it's coming faster than most people think'

— Barry Shenkarow

You see, for all his magic, for all the history and hysteria the Finnish Flash created in his rookie season, even Teemu Selanne couldn't save the Jets.

Looking back, it's rather astonishing that during Selanne's record-busting debut, which generated a media firestorm far beyond the Manitoba borders, the Winnipeg Arena was rarely sold out. In fact, for the most part, crowds were between 12,000 and 13,000. The season-ticket base was never above 6,000. Said Paddock: "It's easy to get caught up in the whiteout stuff (during all-too-brief playoff appearances), but... certainly the attendance wasn't there."

In fact, by the time Selanne arrived in 1992, tentative plans to build a new arena in downtown Winnipeg had been trumpeted

and shelved. In 1990, the Jets' owners, led by president Barry Shenkarow, had signed a deal with the province agreeing to sell the Jets to local buyers for $32 million, provided the provincial government covered the losses for the next five years. During that time, studies would be conducted to determine the viability of a new arena — which Shenkarow had long argued was required to keep the team in Winnipeg.

But health and education budgets were being slashed. The Canadian dollar was in the process of falling to a historic low of 65 cents against the greenback. NHL salaries were just beginning to skyrocket. In 1992, the year Selanne arrived in Winnipeg, the Jets' payroll was $6 million. In the Jets' final season, 1995-96, the team's payroll was just over $20 million.

"Maybe it was just impossible with the dollar exchange," noted Paddock, who in 1994 would take the reins as the Jets' general manager, "but if the movers and shakers and the people with money at the time had put a shovel in the ground... you couldn't have had a better time than after Selanne's first season to get moving in the direction of a new arena. It just wasn't, for whatever reason. It never got to that stage."

As Selanne was taking his first strides as a Jet in September 1992 — and beginning to collect his $2.7-million stipend over three years, Shenkarow was predicting a dire future.

"We are headed for a crisis," he warned, "and I believe it's coming faster than most people think. In the last year, our problems have grown in magnitude to the point where I am afraid for some of the franchises. It's not just Winnipeg that's threatened. Nine or 10 others will be hit just as hard."

Owners wanted a hard salary cap. Players wanted the owners to better share their revenue between larger and small-market teams first, before targeting employee salaries.

It was also in the midst of Selanne's rookie season, February 1993, that the NHL replaced league president Gil Stein with its first commissioner, a New York lawyer named Gary Bettman. Bettman had previously been senior vice-president of the National Basketball Association, which had experienced major growth and stability through the 1980s.

Selanne draws double coverage
in a game against the Detroit Red Wings.

The fatal flaw in the franchise's economic model... was that the owners didn't own the one thing they needed to survive: the arena.

Bettman's mandate was no secret: stem labour unrest and rising salaries and continue the league's initial expansion of "footprints" into non-traditional U.S. markets. The San Jose Sharks had joined the NHL in 1991-92, followed by the Ottawa Senators and Tampa Bay Lightning the following season. In 1993-94, the Minnesota North Stars relocated to Dallas, and the Florida Panthers and Anaheim Mighty Ducks were born.

The Panthers were owned by Blockbuster billionaire Wayne Huizenga, and the Mighty Ducks were founded by the Walt Disney Co.

The NHL was going places, baby. No wonder the small-market Jets, with their antiquated arena and shallow-pocket owners, felt threatened. "It's possible, on a purely economic basis, that Winnipeg isn't big enough for an NHL franchise," Shenkarow said around the time Selanne scored his 35th goal. "It's a big question mark in everybody's mind."

But it wasn't just outside forces that plagued the Jets. The relationship between Shenkarow and the team's landlord, the Winnipeg Enterprises Corp., had gone from dysfunctional to toxic.

The fatal flaw in the franchise's economic model — just as it was dating back to Hatskin — was that the owners didn't own the one thing they needed to survive: the arena.

The WEC, which held a 32 per cent stake in the Jets, reaped all the concessions. Literally. As an entertainment facility, the Winnipeg Arena was a dinosaur in an expansion-crazy era when Disney's state-of-the-art monstrosity in Anaheim would have made the Queen's portrait at the old barn blush.

"Small markets require ideal circumstances in which to survive," Bettman warned. "That means the club has to run as a business. It needs a good broadcasting contract, and it needs a state-of-the-art building that includes club seats, suites, restaurants, parking and concessions. We're in the entertainment business, and part of the package is the building in which the product is presented."

Well, if by "restaurants" Bettman meant hotdog carts outside the building and "suites" meant bare-bones boxes with a mini-fridge, the arena had it all. Meanwhile, Shenkarow's very public feud with the WEC continued unabated.

The Jets get a standing ovation after losing a playoff game to the Detroit Red Wings, 6-1, April 1996.

> **'I don't like it. We've made concessions... given, given, given. The whole time the owners have lied through their teeth and talked out of both sides of their mouth. And now we're supposed to be happy?'**
>
> — veteran Jets defenceman Dean Kennedy, 1993

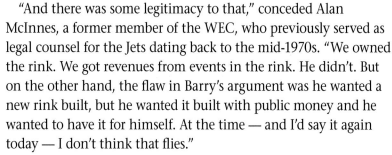

MARC GALLANT WINNIPEG FREE PRESS

"And there was some legitimacy to that," conceded Alan McInnes, a former member of the WEC, who previously served as legal counsel for the Jets dating back to the mid-1970s. "We owned the rink. We got revenues from events in the rink. He didn't. But on the other hand, the flaw in Barry's argument was he wanted a new rink built, but he wanted it built with public money and he wanted to have it for himself. At the time — and I'd say it again today — I don't think that flies."

The final blow for the Winnipeg Jets, in the end, was undoubtedly the owners' lockout that began on Oct. 11, 1994 and ended Jan. 11, 1995, resulting in a shortened 48-game schedule and no shortage of outrage and bitterness that defined and solidified the growing chasm between players, owners and fans.

"It was a new era in sports," Paddock said. "There probably was more cynicism and bitterness toward that kind of money being made, especially in a small market like Winnipeg where you see that person in the grocery store as opposed to places like New York where there was hardly the possibility of getting recognized.

"Then there was all the talk about the team moving and blaming it on the salaries and the so-called greed of the players, or Bettman and the (NHL's economic) system. I don't know. But it was like a nightmare time where as much as the greatness he (Selanne) brought, there weren't any conditions that were positive. It was very unique for sure. It was a horrible era for small-market places like us and Quebec, being the smallest and having the oldest facilities."

Even in the wake of a settlement — which was a crushing blow for the Jets because the owners caved without establishing a salary cap — tempers all around were frayed.

Jets season-ticket holder Peter Valdalos said: "I don't want them (the tickets) at all. I didn't receive the goods, so I cancelled. I lost any interest. It's a funny thing; after so many years, I don't want to see them, I don't miss them. It turned me off, what they (players and owners) did to the people. They had the world by the tail, and they kicked the people out the door. The deal is this: They said to us, 'Go to hell.' So maybe it's time to say the same to them."

Veteran Jets defenceman Dean Kennedy said: "I don't like it. We've made concessions... given, given, given. The whole time the owners have lied through their teeth and talked out of both sides of their mouth. And now we're supposed to be happy?"

Paddock said: "If a player has any animosity, he can hit the road."

And this was after the labour dispute had been settled.

Somewhere in the balcony high in the Winnipeg Arena, the fat lady was clearing her throat.

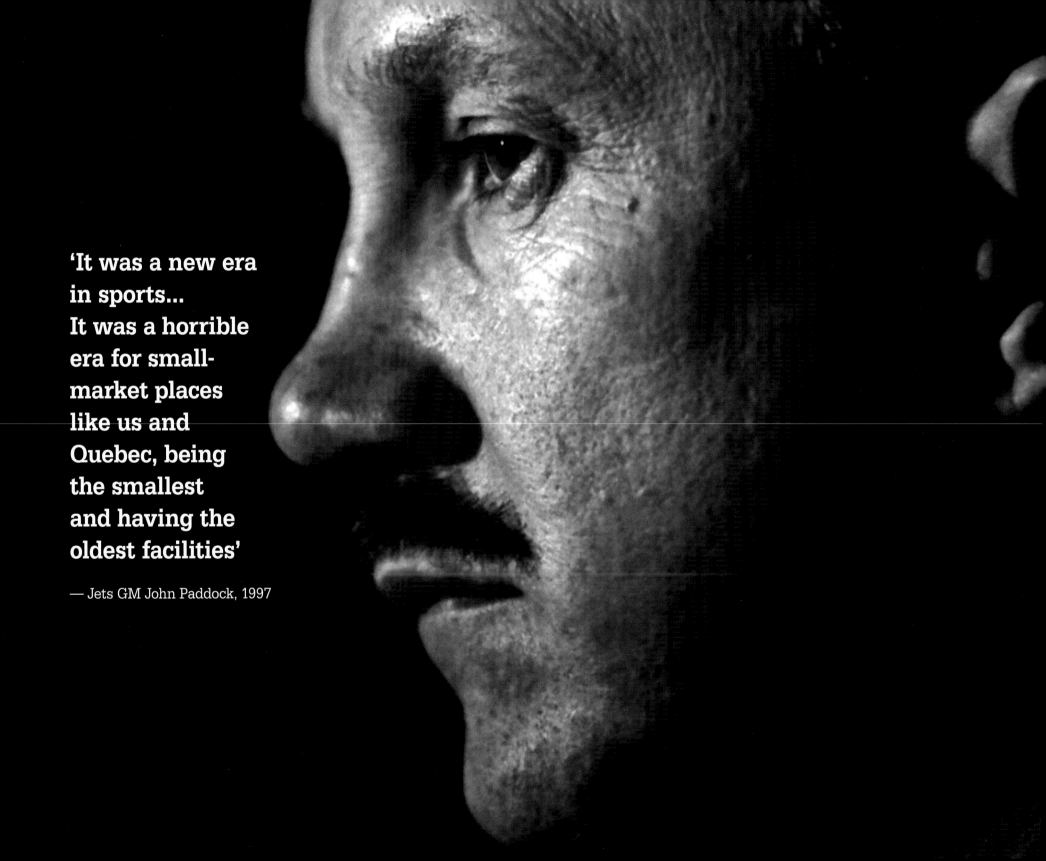

'It was a new era
in sports...
It was a horrible
era for small-
market places
like us and
Quebec, being
the smallest
and having the
oldest facilities'

— Jets GM John Paddock, 1997

Randy Carlyle rushes the puck during Game 4 of a playoff series against the Vancouver Canucks.

KEN GIGLIOTTI WINNIPEG FREE PRESS

But at least the mischievous Selanne never lost his sense of humour. On the night he was presented with the Calder Trophy as 1992-93 rookie of the year, he leaned over to his agent, Baizley, and winked: "Do you think I should thank the Calgary Flames first?"

Alas, Sergei Bautin.

Selanne wasn't the only rookie on the 1992-93 Jets roster. There was also a hulking Russian defenceman who was the anti-Teemu, a first-round pick who, through no fault of his own, came to symbolize the worst of the Mike Smith regime.

It was the 1992 draft and Smith, heavily influenced by the Russian hockey system since attending two seminars in Moscow shortly before joining the Jets staff in 1980, was determined to prove a point: A fast, European puck-possession game was paramount to NHL success in the 1990s.

Smith wasn't necessarily misguided. The Detroit Red Wings proved the point repeatedly in the late '90s and the turn of the 21st century. Unfortunately, Smith drafted too many Artur Oktyabrevs (155th overall in 1992) and not enough Pavel Datsyuks (171st overall in 1998).

But Bautin was the personification of Smith's great Russian experiment. When the Jets announced Bautin's selection, the kid was so low on the NHL draft boards it took TSN analysts 10 minutes to identify him. Smith proclaimed Bautin to be a bone-crushing bruiser and called him the "Jack Tatum of hockey." Not even close. Just weeks into the season, cheeky *Winnipeg Sun* columnist Ed Willes said Smith only got it half-right. "He's the Tatum O'Neal of hockey," Willis scribbled.

Out of a dozen picks in that watershed 1992 draft, Smith selected nine Russians — including a gem in goaltender Nikolai Khabibulin (204th overall in the ninth round).

By then a grizzled veteran just two years from retirement, Randy Carlyle was gobsmacked. Watching the 1992 draft at home, a baffled Carlyle blurted, "'What the (very bad word) is going on?' And I wasn't the only one."

As the saying goes, Carlyle, a Norris Trophy winner with Pittsburgh in 1981, wasn't just old-school. He built the old school. In fact, his attitude, shared at the time by every North American in

Selanne confers with Jets goalie Nikolai Khabibulin between periods in a game against the Chicago Blackhawks.

Netminder
Nikolai Khabibulin

the Jets' dressing room, was identical to that of Joe Daley some two decades before, when he braced for the influx of Swedes and Finns into the WHA Jets in the mid-1970s.

"From our mindset, they (the Russians) were stealing our jobs," Carlyle said. "How else would you look at it? And when there's a mass exodus (in the Smith turnover), it's hard to integrate them into the system when they can't speak the language and don't know the culture. It made it that much more difficult. Believe me, they're good Russian players and good guys. But they weren't like the Swedes and they weren't like the Finns. They were different people. And it took them more time to get acclimated into what was going on. The cultures were at such different ends of the spectrum, so diverse, it made it difficult."

Some of the core aspects of a ruthless, competitive hockey business don't change. Carlyle doesn't apologize for not wholeheartedly accepting the likes of Bautin and fellow countrymen Boris Mironov and Igor Ulanov, all three defencemen.

"If they earned the job, it's fine," Carlyle said. "But you can't be given anything. And that was part of the issue with the Winnipeg Jets. We knew they didn't earn it, but you can't say that. That made it much more difficult for people to accept. So there's resentment, right?"

Smith never shied from his provocative philosophies nor bowed to public sentiment. Just the opposite, in fact.

"What happened was the media attacked him for it," said Carlyle, "and the more they attacked him, the more he would go in that direction."

Carlyle was far from the only disgruntled Jets employee on the ice. Said the ever-diplomatic Steen: "He (Smith) did what was right for him, but I'm not sure what he did was right for everybody else. He drafted some good players, but winning is about a team.

"With so many Europeans it was tough to win, if you know what I mean," Steen added. "We didn't have a tough guy, we had Bautin, and he wasn't a tough guy at the NHL level. So we had a very hard time winning games, even though we had better players than a lot of other teams, because they were beating us up. We had great talent, but we never got all the pieces together. There was always something missing."

Smith did trade for heavyweight Tie Domi and sandpaper forward Kris King, acquired from the New York Rangers to ride shotgun for Selanne & Co. midway through the 1992-93 season and the Jets reeled off 10 straight wins. (King likes to tell the story, tongue-in-cheek, of Rangers GM Neil Smith telling him of the trade: "I've got bad news and worse news," Smith told King. "The bad news is you're being traded to Winnipeg. The worse news is I'm sending Tie Domi with you.")

But even the injection of Broadway muscle was not enough to cure what ailed the Jets in the early 1990s, for all the pure talent of Tkachuk, Selanne, Zhamnov and a fading Steen.

Ultimately, Smith's Russian experiment failed miserably.

In all, Bautin suited up for 130 games with the Jets but simply didn't have the tools to stick in the NHL, much less live up to the first-round billing that epitomized Smith's erudite philosophies. Said Paddock of Bautin: "The poor guy was doomed. He was sort of the poster boy for that draft."

Within two years, Bautin was toiling for the AHL's Adirondack Red Wings. By 2000, he was patrolling the blue-line for the Oji Eagles of the Asian Ice Hockey League.

The Jets didn't fare much better. Back in Winnipeg, the band was breaking up. After three career seasons in Winnipeg, Housley became embroiled in bitter contract negotiations with Smith, who dealt the defenceman to the St. Louis Blues for Nelson Emerson and Stéphane Quintal prior to the start of the 1994-95 season.

"We took a big drop," Paddock said. "Phil Housley wasn't a perfect defenceman, but we missed his game. Big time."

No one missed Housley more than Selanne. After his brilliant rookie season, the Flash never played another full season in a Winnipeg uniform. Selanne missed the bulk of his sophomore season with a sliced Achilles tendon, which threatened his career. Then came the lockout and the lame-duck 1995-96 season, when Paddock, under orders from the Jets' new co-owner, Richard Burke, traded Selanne to the Anaheim Mighty Ducks for defenceman Oleg Tverdovsky, forward Chad Kilger and a third-round draft pick.

MARC GALLANT WINNIPEG FREE PRESS

Phil Housley, No. 6, in a game against the Pittsburgh Penguins.

The Selanne trade was strictly economics: Burke didn't want three forwards each making $3 million a season

Jets coach Terry Simpson reacts to the Teemu Selanne trade in 1996.

The Selanne trade was strictly economics: Burke didn't want three forwards each making $3 million a season, so Paddock had to choose between the Finn, the American (Tkachuk) and the Russian (Zhamnov). Selanne's injury history made him the most expendable. Ironically, Selanne, at age 40, scored 31 goals and added 49 assists for the Ducks in the 2010-11 season. Of the Winnipeg Jets' original Olympic Line, Selanne was the last one standing.

It could be that Winnipeg hockey fans and their franchise were victims of a perfect storm of external and internal forces that conspired against them. The dollar. The salaries. The cynicism. The prevailing sentiment against spending public funds on private arenas.

Clearly, however, fatigue and fat cheques were eroding the collective will to ante up to the NHL's increasingly exorbitant financial demands.

"As the economics started to get seriously out of whack, it became more and more obvious that they weren't going to be able to continue," the WEC's McInnes said. "It was only a matter of time, and unless some sugar daddy stepped up to the plate and bought the team and kept it here — and that person would have to understand there would be losses, not profits, for the most part — it wasn't going to happen.

"There was little prospect of making money as salaries continued to escalate and the dollar was at 64 cents. The point is, businessmen don't go into business to lose money. At a particular point, most people say enough is enough."

At the end of the 1994-95 season, which many believed at the time was the Jets' last call, Shenkarow — long a harbinger of his own hockey team's demise — was well beyond pleas for assistance.

"I have always wanted to keep the team in Winnipeg," he said. "For four years I've provided an offer that is well below market value (C$32 million) but nobody wanted to take me up on it. The business of hockey is a real problem and for us to keep the team in Winnipeg for a year and have someone pick up what could be $15 million or $20 million worth of losses wouldn't be right for anyone. Nobody wants to do that."

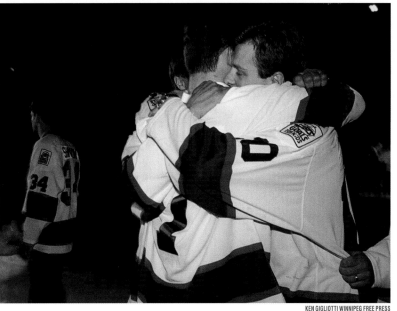

Selanne, Tkachuk and Alexei Zhamnov hug as Jets leave the ice for what they thought would be the last time at the Winnipeg Arena.

KEN GIGLIOTTI WINNIPEG FREE PRESS

Without question, the never-ending financial turmoil and uncertainty surrounding relocation seeped throughout the entire organization. No player or staffer was immune.

"If there's unrest and indecision at the top, that's going to filter down through the organization," Carlyle conceded. "The uneasiness was felt at times: Are we going to be here or not going to be here? Are we going to be sold? New building? No new building? Those are the things that affect the people around you. They don't affect you so much directly because you're consumed with playing, but to say it doesn't ultimately affect you is impossible."

Hence the symbolism attached to Selanne's historic yet abbreviated career as a Winnipeg Jet, which ultimately mirrored the fortunes of his team: from soaring hope (76 goals as a rookie), to cursed setbacks (torn Achilles), to labour unrest (the lockout) to, finally, unworkable economics (the trade to Anaheim).

Yet when the Grim Reaper finally came for the Jets, the emotional outpouring to save the team in the face of every prevailing financial reality — arguably against the community's own economic best interests — was unlike any public display since the great flood of 1950 or the end of two world wars.

When the Grim Reaper finally came for the Jets, the emotional outpouring to save the team in the face of every prevailing financial reality — arguably against the community's own economic best interests — was unlike any public display since the great flood of 1950 or the end of two world wars

Hope can be a beautiful, dangerous thing. That can be the only logical explanation for the extraordinary effort to save such an irretrievably lost cause.

The Jets never won, you see. At least, not enough. From the very beginning, they struggled just to survive — all the way back to the franchise's origins in 1972. Yet somewhere along the way — from Hull's rebellion to Hedberg and Nilsson's revolution to Hawerchuk's renaissance to Selanne's revelation — an invisible bond had been formed.

The Jets were never perfect. Even as champions, they were outlaws and outcasts. In the NHL, they were, at times, also-rans and afterthoughts. Almost always they were left wanting in the shadows of greatness or just one stride behind the men who would eventually drink from the Stanley Cup.

But they were Winnipeg's team, even if the city didn't always want them enough. So when the end came, the realization of what would be lost was intensified. Even exaggerated.

It didn't matter if it was a billionaire or a babysitter, the passion to hold onto the Jets — or the idea of the Jets — would reach staggering heights and gut-wrenching emotional depths.

Even though it was far too late, they tried.

Lord, how they tried.

NHL commissioner Gary Bettman was under police protection when he came to Winnipeg on April 29, 1995 to discuss the possible sale of the Jets.

Jets owner Barry Shenkarow looks sombre during the press conference announcing the Jets would likely leave Winnipeg.

JOE BRYKSA WINNIPEG FREE PRESS

Winnipeg Fi

60 PAGES
VOL 123 NO 148
CANADA POST SALES
AGREEMENT NO. 563595

c

Friday, April 28

Outrage! Winnipeg Jets fans lash back after 11th-hour demands by the NHL dash their hopes for a new arena and a competitive franchise.

Winnipeg needs its Jets. Economically, it's a huge loss.
— Kevin Palmer.

Shafted b

'A bullet through the heart of Winnipeg'

By Nick Martin and John Douglas
Staff Reporters

THE WINNIPEG Jets are as good as dead unless the NHL backs down on a list of tough demands it made just 72 hours before a deadline to find new owners for the hockey club.

Provincial and civic politicians demanded Prime Minister Chretien move to save Canada's national game. CJOB host Peter Warren called for a mass demonstration this morning at Portage Avenue and Main Street.

All levels of government called

The newspaper clipping reads:

ce Press

00¢ + GST + PST outside city
75¢ in Ontario

Weekly home delivery
$3.25 wkly ($3.05 + 20 PST) in Winnipeg
$3.30 wkly ($3.09 + 21 PST) outside city

"...and fans, given the businessmen
...and we cannot give any more. It's
...time for the NHL to stop this and
...look at what this sport means to
...all of us."
— Ann Crawford

the NHL

Demands 'outrageous,' Loewen says

By John Douglas
Business Reporter

IT WAS an ambush.
That's how Manitoba Entertainment Complex chairman John Loewen put it yesterday after receiving a letter from the NHL and making "outrageous and unreasonable" demands on the group trying to keep the Jets in town.

"I didn't get the letter until today," he said in an interview. "We're 72 hours from a deadline and the league moves to undermine everything we've done to date."

In a letter to the prospective Jets owners, NHL commissioner Gary Bettman said the league would not allow the team to be resold until it ... at least $25 million in the ...

■ Jets plan crashes, burns /C1
■ Maybe this thing's not over /C1
■ It's not the end of the world /C3

Manitoba Finance Minister Eric Stefanson fired the puck back at the league.

"The true test of the NHL will be whether they are sincere about keeping hockey in Winnipeg and other small-market teams," he said.

The MEC was formed to keep the team in Winnipeg long-term but the plan has always allowed for an escape clause if losses over five, six or seven years increased dramatically. If that was the case, the ownership would sell the team and use the proceeds to pay off all arena debts.

The NHL demand means the ownership would be forced to finance ... for a decade without an es-

---

CHAPTER SEVEN:

The Jets Crash

THE Winnipeg Jets didn't just drop dead. If only.

They lingered.

The torture wasn't just to see the team dying; it was to see it succumb, then show a faint pulse, then give up the ghost again.

Indeed, if there is a hell for sports fans, the seventh circle was reserved for the Jets' most passionate fans as the team went through its throes.

In the spring of 1995, all last-ditch efforts by local governments and a hodgepodge of business leaders to raise the $32 million required to purchase the Jets from team owner Barry Shenkarow — subject to the approval of the National Hockey League overlords — had been torturously exhausted.

Dancing Gabe Langlois, in Jets jersey, a mainstay in all Winnipeg sports, took part in the rally at Portage and Main on April 28, 1995.

At the same time, NHL commissioner Gary Bettman was distancing the league from the Jets' interminable stretch on death row.

"This is not an NHL decision," Bettman insisted to the *Toronto Star* on May 3, 1995. "This is really up to the people in Winnipeg and the prospective owners... to see if there's something to be done to keep the team there. But the biggest problem is there doesn't seem to be anybody, in a serious fashion, who wants to own the franchise."

Days later, in an interview with the *Globe and Mail*, the commissioner pointed out that teams in Hartford, Quebec City, Winnipeg and Edmonton were not chosen by the league for expansion but absorbed during the WHA/NHL merger. Bettman suggested that, given the growth of professional sports as industries since 1979, such small markets didn't have the money and population to keep pace.

As the Jets withered, there was rumbling the team could end up in Atlanta — or even the Arizona desert.

In February 1995, a headline appeared in the *Toronto Star*: "Phoenix awaits Canadian NHL flop."

With the NHL's overt efforts to focus on U.S. "footprints" while the Jets and other Canadian small-market teams fought for survival, the mood in Winnipeg was evolving from concern to fear and ultimately to open hostility.

The bitterness was rampant. When negotiations cratered in late April, a headline as thick as a 32-ounce steak on the front page of the *Free Press* screamed: "Shafted by the NHL."

A large crowd blocked traffic at Portage and Main for the Save the Jets rally.

Thomas
Steen

Cue the mobs at Portage and Main, where 35-year-old Jerry Simpson showed up cradling his two-year-old daughter. "She watches hockey every Saturday night with me," Simpson said. "We cheer the goals of the Jets and I wanted to share the death of the NHL in Winnipeg with her."

The mood was maudlin. It was sentimental. It was angry.

"They've put a bullet through the heart of Winnipeg," said fan Chris Walters.

The venom wasn't confined to the street. Accusations were flying at the highest levels. Premier Gary Filmon was getting death threats on his answering machine. At home.

"People went wild," Filmon recalled. "Everybody was in chaos. The emotional output was so intense, the only thing that came close to it was Meech Lake. I was a little bit concerned about my family, because they were saying that people were saying things to them. You just worried about those things, whether somebody could do something really stupid."

At the end, the feeling among all parties involved was barely veiled hostility.

Then-Winnipeg mayor Susan Thompson remembers the key players gathering in the Westin Hotel's Royal Suite, minutes before a press conference officially announcing the Jets were gone.

"It was an absolute funeral," Thompson recalled. "Nobody spoke. Not a word. The room was as quiet as quiet can be. I can't remember who I tried to approach, but they just turned away."

Then it got worse.

At the press conference, Thompson broke down. "I don't know if it was exhaustion or losing the team," she recalled. "I got up and my voice cracked. I couldn't hold it. I cried. I cried on CNN."

So did Shenkarow. Even former Jets great Thomas Steen, who had retired the previous season after 14 distinguished years in a Jets uniform, bolted from the room in tears.

Filmon was stone-faced at the podium, however.

"And everybody asked me why I didn't cry," Filmon said, years later.

"Why not?" someone asked.

"Because tears wouldn't help," Filmon replied.

WINNIPEG ARENA

WINNIPEG ARENA
HOME OF THE WINNIPEG JETS

I'm a K.L. Believer in the Winnipeg Jets Thank You

Fans gather to mourn the loss of the Jets.

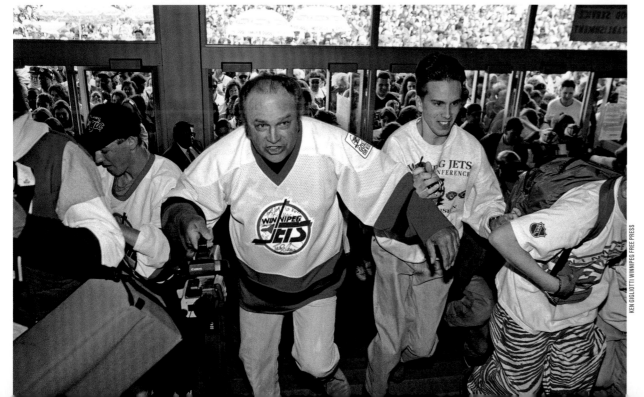

Rushing for good seats at the final gathering at the Winnipeg Arena to say goodbye to the Jets. The day became known as The Funeral.

More than 15,000 people attending the Funeral to honour the Jets watch as a banner marking their days in Winnipeg is raised to the rafters of the Winnipeg Arena.

Nothing would. For all the complex, emotionally charged and ultimately futile negotiations, it was a simple matter of unworkable economics. Shenkarow didn't want the team, which was beginning to hemorrhage millions in losses — with no new arena on the horizon — and no one in the community was willing to ante up the $32-million asking price and absorb the subsequent losses.

Besides, Shenkarow had a $65-million offer on the table from Minneapolis businessmen Richard Burke and Steven Gluckstern. That was US$65 million, worth a cool C$100 million at the time. There were no other viable options. Not for Shenkarow and certainly not for the NHL.

Three days later, a ceremony was held at the Winnipeg Arena. It was grimly dubbed the Funeral.

The notion was honourable — to retire Steen's jersey and say

a tearful goodbye to the team, then believed to be bound for Minnesota.

But no one was kidding himself, not even the soft-spoken Steen, who had to be rushed to hospital during a luncheon prior to the ceremony. The toll of recent days had been too much for the graceful centreman.

"He fainted," recalled Jets teammate Randy Gilhen. "It was an emotional time for him. It all caught up to him — the stress and lack of sleep, the anxiety of thinking the team was moving."

Steen recovered to attend the ceremony. His No. 25 jersey was raised into the rafters along with another banner — Winnipeg Jets: 1972-1995.

Don Cherry was a surprise guest, and he bellowed: "They made a big mistake here, I'll tell you that. They might have taken

Winnipeg Free Press

32 PAGES
VOL. 132 NO. 157
CANADA POST SALES
AGREEMENT NO. 560936

50¢

Sunday, May 7, 1995

Farewell, Jets

Steen, mates get teary sendoff

By Ashley Prest
Sports Reporter

THEY SAID it with tears, with cheers and with banners but in the end, Winnipeg Jets fans said goodbye with class.

More than 15,000 hockey fans made it a day to remember yesterday, packing the Winnipeg Arena to bid a final farewell to the players and coaches of the National Hockey League team, which is officially for sale and expected to leave the city.

They also came to honor veteran Jets forward Thomas Steen, whose No. 25 was retired after 14 years — his entire NHL career — with the Jets.

Many of the fans wore white, as they did in past playoff games.

Some waved banners, some shook white pom-poms and some whistled. All cheered wildly as a Winnipeg Jets banner with the dates 1972-1995 was raised to the rafters by Ab McDonald, the first Jets captain, assistant coach Randy Carlyle and Randy Gilhen, a Winnipeg native who scored the last Jets goal.

Then Steen's No. 25 was hoisted by captain Keith Tkachuk and defenceman Dave Manson.

Don Cherry, a surprise guest from Hockey Night in Canada, surveyed the crowd and voiced the injustice that everyone in the arena felt was being done to Winnipeg.

"They made a big mistake here, I'll tell you that," Cherry bellowed. "They might have taken your franchise, but they haven't taken your heart and soul.

"You're the greatest."

The doors opened at 12:30 p.m. and 30 minutes later the lower section of seats was full. By 12:55, people were on their feet chanting, "Save our Jets."

There were plenty of banners in the crowd.

"First Gretzky, then Barry."

What's the Future of Hockey in Canada?

Fans got to remember the Jets' proud past when McDonald and other old-timers, along with some staff and players were introduced.

General Manager John Paddock and several players addressed the crowd, praising the loyalty and warmth of the fans.

Forward Ed Olczyk got the loudest reaction.

"I would like to walk to all the sides out there who are Jets fans and I understand just what you're saying," he told the hundreds of fans lined up outside the Arena yesterday, waiting for the doors to open.

'No more dreaming of next year'

By Randy Turner
Sports Reporter

IT WAS last call in the Winnipeg Arena and Jason Devisser was staring at an empty sheet of ice in the near-deserted building, long after it had fallen silent.

The Winnipeg Jets had left, never to return, but Devisser could not.

"I know I'm not accomplishing anything by sitting here," said Devisser, 22. "But I just don't want to leave, because that's when it will really sink in.

"I've got so many things going through my mind. I don't believe it. I've had so many good memories here over the years."

Such was the sombre scene yesterday afternoon, shortly after more than 15,000 Jets fans crammed into the Arena to lay their hockey team to rest.

It was an emotional farewell. Jennifer Hanson sang the national anthem one last time. On the loudspeaker, Stompin' Tom Connors crooned the Hockey Game song.

When the Jets took to the ice, they were greeted with a thunderclap of applause. Somebody started the wave.

Just like the old days.

But even as they celebrated the past, the anger and frustration of many fans was never too far from the surface.

Thomas Steen's jersey wasn't the only thing hung up yesterday. Three fans arrived at the farewell with effigies of Premier Gary Filmon hanging from hockey sticks.

"The team could have been saved," said Brad Henry, who accused Filmon of using the Jets to win last month's election.

"Filmon had a chance to do it."

"I think people should keep pushing the politicians until they get some answers," said Devisser, who believes an arena-casino concept could have saved the club.

"We can't reach him now, eh?" said Ian Lee to Marilyn.

When Hanson belted out and left the Arena, she was dabbing red roses with a Kleenex.

"It's that last ol' roll call," she said. "I miss you a great deal, Jets.

"I feel orange."

Steen (left) kisses his wife while teammates Darrin Shannon (top right) and Teppo Numminen prepare to raise his No. 25 to the rafters.

Complete coverage
- The story in pictures /A5
- From depths to the rafters /C1
- A part of Winnipeg dies /C3

WE WILL NEVER FORGET JETS

GOOD BYE AND GOOD LUCK

Thomas Steen holds the banner with his number, 25, before it is raised to the rafters of the Winnipeg Arena on May 6, 1995.

Jets wave to their fans after the final game of the 1995 season, a game they thought would be their last in the Winnipeg Arena.

Fans take to the ice after the final buzzer to end the Jets' last game of the 1995 season.

Centreman Ed Olczyk speaks to the crowd of 15,000 at the 1995 goodbye to the Jets.

your franchise, but not your heart and soul." Veteran forward Ed Olcyzk vowed: "We'll always be Winnipeg Jets. Wherever this team ends up, when we win a Stanley Cup, it's coming back to Winnipeg!"

An hour after the entire Jets team raised their hockey sticks to the crowd and left the ice, there were fans who refused to leave their seats in a deserted, silent building. When fan Diana Semchyshyn left the arena, she was dabbing red eyes with a Kleenex.

"It's real sad, a real loss," she said. "It's dead now. They're gone. There's nothing more to it."

Added Brad Henry, one of the other 15,000-plus in attendance: "There's no more dreaming of next year. There is no next year."

If only Henry had been right. There would have been so much less suffering.

But hope dies hard on the Prairies, and there remained a belief that one man in Winnipeg could emerge through a billow of his own nicotine smoke to come to the Jets' rescue: media mogul and self-made billionaire Izzy Asper, who in the mid-1990s was in the process of amassing his CanWest empire.

Asper didn't even like hockey and had never watched the Jets play. But his sons, Leonard and David, had urged Izzy to make an 11th-hour attempt to buy the Jets from Shenkarow.

Asper was initially recruited when Bob Chipman, Mark Chipman's father and the patriarch of the Chipman auto and property-management businesses, phoned him and said, "Izzy, Gary Filmon wants to meet with you to talk about the Jets." Then Chipman picked up the phone and called the premier. "Gary, Izzy wants to meet with you to talk about the Jets."

When Asper met with Filmon in the cabinet room of the legislative building to help formulate a plan to save the team, he barked, "Get me an ashtray."

Izzy Asper, executive chairman of CanWest Global Communications, and Winnipeg Mayor Susan Thompson enter a meeting with city councillors on May 16, 1995 to talk about saving the Jets. Thompson is wearing a blue Save the Jets ribbon on her lapel.

KEN GIGLIOTTI WINNIPEG FREE PRESS

Jets beat Red Wings despite announcement

Players stunned by news

By Tim Campbell and Randy Turner
Sports Reporters

BY NOW, you've already realized that today's news about hockey, the Winnipeg Jets and the NHL is all about business.

Jets 4 Red Wings 3

Well, after the Jets took care of their own situation on Winnipeg Arena ice last night with a 4-3 victory over the Detroit Red Wings, they admitted being stunned and frustrated by news that Manitoba Entertainment Complex Inc. has decided their deal to keep the team in Winnipeg in a new facility just won't fly.

"All the guys love this city," said Jets winger Kris King, who contributed a goal to last night's victory. "We don't want to leave. We're still clinging to that little bit of hope.

"I think the news actually helped the team. It seemed to bring the guys together."

Jets coach Terry Simpson addressed the subject of the the MEC announcement in his pre-game remarks, because the story was about two hours...

By winning — and sending the league-leading Wings to their second straight loss for the first time this season — the Jets pulled into a tie with San Jose and Los Angeles in ninth place in the Western Conference. The Edmonton Oilers beat the St. Louis Blues 3-2 last night to move into sole possession of eighth place — the final playoff spot.

"I mean, how can you not think about it and wonder what's going on," said forward Nelson Emerson. "You've got your families and kids in school and you wonder where you're going to be employed next year. I don't think it's over yet."

Jets GM John Paddock, a native Manitoban, said last night he couldn't separate his feelings from his job.

"That's a very upsetting announcement at the time and if it does go that way, people from Manitoba have a lot to deal with internally, like the people in our office," Paddock said. "That's very tough for Manitoba, people involved in this hockey team."

Paddock also marvelled...

Premier Gary Filmon
(left) and businessman
John Loewen address
the crowd at the April 28,
1995 Save the Jets rally
that had moved to the
Manitoba legislature from
Portage and Main.

The premier politely informed Asper it was, you know, a non-smoking building.

"If you want me to solve this problem," Asper told the premier, "get me an ashtray."

Said Filmon, a lifelong Jets fan: "Bring him an ashtray."

Izzy lit a Craven A king-size.

The plan was straightforward, on the surface: Filmon would try to get the city and the feds on board to pay for a new $111-million downtown arena. Asper was going to try to raise $32 million to buy the Jets and another $50 to $100 million for a fund to cover, in perpetuity, any losses the team would suffer.

Word of Asper's intervention stirred not just optimism, but an unprecedented grassroots campaign that literally had Winnipeggers flocking into the streets for impromptu donation

More than 30,000 people showed up at a Save the Jets rally at The Forks May 16, 1995.

A limousine tows a float carrying CJOB host Peter Warren and others, part of yet another rally at Portage and Main on May 18, 1995.

drives. A rally at The Forks, 35,000 strong, had generated pledges totalling $100,000. Mark Olson's social at the Winnipeg Convention Centre raised more than $200,000.

Vic Grant, the old Jets beat writer who was then director of programming at radio station CJOB, could scarcely believe his eyes.

"I remember we put (longtime CJOB personality) Peter Warren on a wagon and sent him down Portage Avenue and people would throw their money at him," Grant chortled. "Piggy banks. That showed the passion of the people of Winnipeg."

So it was that on May 18, 1995, the city's delirious hockey fans once again gathered en masse at Portage and Main. They had done their part and now they were breathlessly awaiting a noon deadline where Asper would triumphantly announce that his attempts to raise the millions needed to revive their beloved hockey team had succeeded.

They were high-fiving each other in the streets. Total strangers were hugging each other. Stompin' Tom Connors' *Good Old Hockey Game* was blaring over the loudspeakers.

The poor souls.

Up on the 31st floor of Canwest headquarters, the valiant, doomed effort to persuade local businessmen to risk their personal wealth and that of their children on a professional hockey team burning millions in the NHL's smallest market was too much of an ask. And everybody in the room knew it, too.

It was a meeting where money talked. One of the less well-heeled businessmen in the room recalled, "It was nerve-racking. I remember wanting to say something, but feared to."

Why?

"We were punks. That's what they (the bigger fish) thought of us. If you wanted to speak up, put your hand in your pocket. There was an attitude like, 'You little f--kers. Are you in or are you out? Because I'm in and if you're not, get the hell out of the room.'" Such was the tension level when Asper looked around that boardroom that day and asked the critical question, "Who's in?"

Tyler and Ashlee Peacock donate $11.69 to help save the Jets. They were not the only children who emptied out their piggy banks to help.

Bob Silver was in the Canwest conference room as it became obvious the Jets would not be saved.

Coughing. Silence. The faint echo of, "Hello, out there, we're on the air, it's hockey night tonight. Tension grows, the whistle blows, the puck goes down the ice... "

Mark Chipman was in the conference room, one of the group of young Turks, as they were dubbed, who were instrumental in the last-ditch Save the Jets efforts. He remembers the voices rising up from the street like eerie background noises to the jagged-edged tension in the boardroom.

"I could hear *Good Old Hockey Game* pounding," Chipman said. "I remember that very vividly. The irony of that really hit me — that there were these people that, myself included, were so passionately desirous that this was going to come together, and obviously it wasn't going to."

Bob Silver, the owner of Western Glove Works, who would in a few years become co-owner of the *Winnipeg Free Press*, was on the 31st floor, too, watching the noon deadline come and go, unanswered. Silver found the scene surreal and unforgettable.

"They (the fans below) were probably thinking all their pennies and all their dollars and millions of dollars in donations had saved the day," he said. "It was like those people were down there celebrating a win in a horse race, but we were looking at the photo finish. And we lost."

The rest was the long goodbye. In August 1995, Shenkarow officially announced the team would be sold to Gluckstern and Burke, but spend the upcoming season in Winnipeg. And while Shenkarow was widely viewed at the time as a culprit by a constituency of the disgruntled masses — there were enough black hats to go around — the fact was nobody else, in the end, was willing to risk the untold losses, either.

Longtime Jets veterans, in particular Randy Carlyle and Thomas Steen, did not join in the criticism of Shenkarow. In fact, Carlyle argues that you can't knock Shenkarow's influence on the franchise while at the same time acknowledging the strengths Ferguson embodied in the team.

"You need ownership who has the same vision," Carlyle noted. "There's a bad man in all of this who never gets any credit. There's a villain in a lot of people's minds, but he's the guy who wrote the cheques and spent the money to bring people in. He's the guy who believed in what Fergie was doing.

"He was viewed by a lot of people as the one who sold out. But it was in a no-win situation. He made a decision that any businessman would make today. To me, it's awful, the perception of a villain who sold the team. He's a businessman and he did what he had to do. In the end, he had to sell the hockey club because it wasn't fiscally responsible to keep it there. At least, that's my perception."

Steen, meanwhile, believes that the deeply embedded, bitter feelings created by the loss of the Jets still haunt Shenkarow to this day.

"It didn't matter what you said to people, they needed somebody to blame," he said. "But it wasn't his fault. He said all these things way ahead of time and nobody would listen. Then it happened. It's been hurting him really bad. Because our relationship before that day was very good. Afterwards it's good, too, but it's very hard to talk to him about any of this stuff. That's sad, because we really want him to know it wasn't his fault."

The final Jets season had an air of quiet indignity. In early February 1996, beloved superstar Teemu Selanne was dealt to the Anaheim Mighty Ducks for the immortal Chad Kilger, Oleg Tverdovsky and some draft picks Winnipeg fans would never get to see. Insult, meet injury.

The tears had long since dried, and once it was revealed that the Jets' new home would be in Phoenix, Ariz., — yet another "footprint" in Bettman's master plan — the final kick to the gut of a prone body already curled up in the fetal position had been delivered.

For GM John Paddock, the fact that the Jets managed to qualify for the 1996 post-season with a modest 36-40-6 record was a minor miracle in itself. "That year was one of the most amazing in sports," he said. "Because we knew we were a lame duck. So to get a team like that into the playoffs I think is one of the more remarkable accomplishments (in Jets history)."

That's because many in the organization were dying a little each day, especially a small-town Manitoba guy like Paddock.

Zhamnov (from left), Steen and Selanne skate around the Winnipeg Arena ice waving goodbye to fans at the end of the Funeral on May 6, 1995.

Born.
Died:
R.I.P.

By Bill Redekop
Staff Reporter

SO LONG, Winnipeg
There will never be a
you.

A sellout crowd of more t
15,500 fans said a final goo
to their professional hockey
yesterday, as the Detroit R
Wings eliminated the Jets f
the National Hockey Leagu
Stanley Cup playoffs with
victory. The powerful Wing
the best-of-seven Western
ference quarter-final serie
games to two.

The Jets will move to Ph
Ariz. next season.

A half-hour after the fina
buzzer, thousands of Jets f

Hundreds of fans poured onto the ice after the Detroit Red Wings beat the Jets yesterday.

re Jets coverage/ **D1, D3**

inside the arena. Many sat
nless in their seats. A cou-
hundred others milled
d on the ice.
as an emotional afternoon
n and women, both young
d, shed tears as their 24-
ove affair with the Jets
to an end.
l Mauro, 74, wasn't ashamed
dewy eyes.
e been a hockey fan ever
I was a youngster," he
ined.
elve-year-old Courtney Mar-
derstood.

nued
see **JETS/A2**

The Jets accept a
standing ovation and
shake hands with fans
after their final game
of 1995.

"To come home, basically within three hours of where you were born and manage an NHL team, it couldn't be any more of a dream come true," he said. "To be part of it when they had to leave... It was hard."

Still, there was the last call. The Jets were to face the powerful Detroit Red Wings in the first playoff round and the chance to experience one more whiteout, no matter how bittersweet, was too enticing for the faithful to ignore.

The post-season only prolonged the inevitable. The Jets fell behind in the series 3-1 but rallied in Game 5 to steal a 3-1 victory on the back of Russian netminder Nikolai Khabibulin. Back in Winnipeg for Game 6, the arena was jammed to the rafters and trembling. The atmosphere was a curious mixture of joy and inevitable doom, like Slim Pickens riding the atom bomb, whooping and hollering all the way down, in the final scene of *Dr. Strangelove*.

Jordy Douglas, briefly a Jet himself, was the radio analyst for the team on CJOB that night. In all his winters in hockey rinks around North America, Douglas had never before heard such noise as the arena clock ticked down on a 4-1 Wings victory in Game 6.

"Honest to God, we didn't say anything on air," Douglas recalled. "I remember the deafening noise in the old barn. It was dripping

with emotion. To me — and this is going to sound a little crazy — it was almost like an animal in pain. That was my interpretation. It wasn't like a 'thank you for a great season' cheer. It was like a wounded animal crying out a 'save me' kind of cheer. We weren't talking. There was nothing to say. That sound spoke volumes."

In the season that ended just before that fateful May 18 meeting, the Jets' payroll was $13 million. The league average was $16 million, with the Los Angeles Kings leading the spenders at $24.3 million. The Ottawa Senators were the most frugal at $9.4 million.

By 2003-04, the last season before the NHL's historic lockout and salary-cap settlement, payrolls averaged $44 million, from Florida's low of $26.4 million to $77 million for the New York Rangers.

"On reflection... if we got the building built... it would have been a painful experience to live in the NHL economics for the last 10 years," said Chipman. "I can tell you that in the business plans that were drafted under proposals to keep the team here (in 1995), we did not contemplate in any way, shape or form the escalation in salaries that occurred. We would have been awash in red ink.

"So while it was deeply disappointing at the time... maybe we needed to sit out until the league got its house in order."

Added Filmon: "Nobody had those deep pockets (in Winnipeg) that could have sustained those losses. I think everybody is

The Winnipeg Arena, home of the Jets, was imploded on March 26, 2006. Giant excavating machines finished the job.

KEN GIGLIOTTI WINNIPEG FREE PRESS

Head coach Wayne Gretzky behind the Phoenix Coyotes' bench and Shane Doan, No. 19, as the final minutes tick past in a game against the Detroit Red Wings Oct. 11, 2006.

breathing a sigh of relief, 'Boy, are we ever glad (we didn't buy the team).' "

Still, it's not that the Jets just up and died, either. They're living under an assumed name in Phoenix. And while most remnants of the Jets are long gone, traded or retired, their lineage could be heard for the longest time in the husky tones of Coyotes play-by-play man Curt Keilback. In fact, every time Stuart Murray heard that voice, the old roadie was reminded of the words from that Joni Mitchell classic *Big Yellow Taxi*: "You don't know what you've got till it's gone."

On an overcast morning on March 26, 2006, almost a decade after the Jets played their final game, they levelled the Winnipeg Arena with 200 sticks of dynamite...

And put up a parking lot.

ACTUALLY, the dynamite didn't exactly "level" the Winnipeg Arena.

She went down fighting to the bitter end. The explosion brought down the outer shell, but the foundation of concrete pillars and steel girders stubbornly remained standing.

That's when the phone of longtime Jets trainer Craig Heisinger rang. It was Keith Tkachuk, wondering what was causing the delay.

"Are you chained to it or what?" Tkachuk asked, chortling.

The suggestion wasn't without merit. Heisinger was born and raised in Winnipeg, and in his youth the aspiring goalie had spent hours in the arena, sneaking into old WHA games to watch his idols such as Jets mainstay Joe Daley and Mike Liut of the Hartford Whalers. He'd sneak into wrestling matches and concerts.

"I grew up in that building," Heisinger said. "I knew every nook and cranny of that place."

In the mid-'80s, John Ferguson hired Heisinger as an assistant trainer, and within a year, the diminutive hockey lifer was head trainer. He spent 11 seasons with the Jets, honing his craft to the point where superstars such as Paul Coffey and Wayne Gretzky, the Jets' hated opponents, would trust nobody but Heisinger with their skate repairs. (In case you're wondering, it was allowed. Equipment managers have to make a buck, too.)

Heisinger bled Jets colours, and when talk began to surface in the early 1990s about the team's uncertain future, Heisinger, in his early 30s, was convinced his days in his hometown were numbered.

But a funny thing happened to Heisinger's plans: He got married to his wife, Vickie, and they soon found themselves raising four boys: Jake, Mack, Tucker and Zachery.

So when the curtain fell on the Jets in late April 1996, Heisinger had made the hard decision to stay behind rather than uproot his young family for the Arizona desert. He was virtually the only one left behind. Management was leaving, the staff was leaving, the players were leaving.

Then came the last night, when the Red Wings eliminated the Jets in Game 6, and the arena had been emptied. The players, who had silently sat in their stalls absorbing the finality, had gone. The fans, who lingered long after the final whistle to say their goodbyes, had vanished into the night.

Only Heisinger was left, a solitary figure vacuuming the carpet of the Jets' dressing room with tears in his eyes.

"Clear as day," Heisinger said, when asked if he remembered the moment. "I hadn't thought about it for a long time. It's the end of an era, when you're emotionally tied to something for a long period of time. We'd lost. The team was leaving. Everybody else was gone. The gear was hung. You knew it was over."

Earlier, Coffey, a veteran with the Wings, had dropped by the Winnipeg dressing room to personally thank Heisinger and wish him well. "That was hard," the trainer said. "He gave me a hug and we moved on."

The irony was not lost on Heisinger. "I thought if the team left, I'd be the first one out of here," he said. "But the team was leaving and I was the only one staying."

Heisinger had a new job: equipment manager for the Manitoba Moose of the International Hockey League, which had the unenviable task of arriving on Winnipeg's doorstep, only to be greeted with all the warmth of an unwanted orphan.

That's where Moose owner Mark Chipman and Heisinger started — at the bottom, with a minor-league hockey team that only reminded disgruntled, mourning Jets fans of what they'd lost.

The air was thick with bad karma. For the Moose, everything had to be perfect. Said Chipman: "You only get one chance to make a good first impression."

And then it all went horribly wrong.

Only Heisinger was left, a solitary figure vacuuming the carpet of the Jets' dressing room with tears in his eyes...
'We'd lost.
The team was leaving.
Everybody else was gone.
The gear was hung.
You knew it was over'

Heisinger in his role of equipment manager for the Manitoba Moose in December 1998.

Jets players celebrate
a playoff goal against
the Detroit Red Wings
in front of a famed
"white out" crowd
on April 21, 1996

SUMMER 1979

After paying $6 million in franchise fees, each WHA team would be allowed to protect only two goalies and two skaters. The Jets protect Morris Lukowich and Scott Campbell, then considered the next Larry Robinson by some, but lose Kent Nilsson, Terry Ruskowski, Rich Preston, Barry Long and Kim Clackson. Forced to pick at the back of the entry draft of juniors, the Jets goof by taking Jimmy Mann 19th overall — just ahead of Michel Goulet and Kevin Lowe, although they do snag Dave Christian in the second round and Thomas Steen and Tim Watters in the fifth and sixth rounds.

"It is not what they are that will bother Winnipeg hockey fans," writes *Free Press* columnist Hal Sigurdson as the new, but completely ravaged team prepared for its first season in the NHL. "It is what they were. And what they might have been."

OCT. 10, 1979

The Jets make their NHL debut in a 4-2 loss to the Pittsburgh Penguins at the Igloo. The Jets' first-ever NHL goal came from the stick of Morris Lukowich — although the dispute still rages that Peter Marsh should get credit, not just an assist. Peter Sullivan has the other, and management seems pleased with the effort of the ragtag lot.

"You must realize that we're on a long journey," says Tom McVie. "We've just got packed, and we're starting off on the same road together. Some clubs never get started. Guys are going north, others south, some east and others west.

"But we're all headed in the same direction."

OCT. 14, 1979

The Jets make their NHL home debut and pick up their first win, a 4-2 decision over Don Cherry and the Colorado Rockies in front of 12,619 at an expanded Winnipeg Arena.

The Jets finish their inaugural NHL season with a record of 20-49-11 — tied with Colorado for worst in the league but with one more win than the Rockies.

OCT. 19-DEC. 20, 1980

Welcome to the Jets' nightmare and a streak that still stands in the record books for futility. Winnipeg opens the 1980-81 season with two losses before knocking off the Black Hawks 6-2 in their home opener. What begins next is a journey so awful it was documented in *Sports Illustrated* — a winless streak that stretches over 30 games with 23 losses and seven ties. It costs McVie his job as he is fired on Dec. 11 and ends Dec. 23, 1980 with a 5-4 win over Colorado.

"You should have seen the room when the players first came in after the game," says Billy Sutherland, who had replaced Tom McVie. "It was like they'd won the Stanley Cup."

The Jets finish the season 9-57-14, one more than the expansion 1974-75 Washington Capitals.

JUNE 10, 1981- AUG. 13, 1981

The Jets find the new face of the franchise in Cornwall Royals centre Dale Hawerchuk, drafted first overall and signed at the corner of Portage and Main — à la Hull in 1972 — in mid-August.

The signing draws 800 people and Joey Gregorash writes a song for the event. "Imagine," says Gus Badali, Hawerchuk's agent, "he's been in town for two days and already there's a song about him."

Hawerchuk earns every bit of his five-year, $800,000 contract in Year 1, leading the Jets to a second-place finish while scoring 45 goals, adding 58 assists and being named the NHL's top rookie.

The Jets qualify for the playoffs for the first time, but fall 3-1 in a best-of-five series loss to the St. Louis Blues.

APRIL 14, 1985

The Jets knock off the Calgary Flames 5-3 at the Saddledome to win their first NHL playoff series. Two significant developments from that series: 1. On April 10, 1985 the Jets beat the Flames 5-4 at the arena in the first-ever whiteout. 2. Three days later, on April 13, 1985, Hawerchuk is cross-checked by Jamie Macoun and misses the rest of the playoffs, including a four-game sweep by the eventual champion Edmonton Oilers in the next round.

That season, the Jets go 43-27-10 for 96 points, their best season in Winnipeg, and Hawerchuk is the runner-up to Wayne Gretzky for the Hart Trophy as the NHL MVP.

APRIL 16, 1987

The Jets hammer the Calgary Flames 6-1 at the Winnipeg Arena to win their second — and last — Stanley Cup playoff series. As per usual, they run into the Edmonton Oilers in the second round and are swept in four straight. The Oilers advance to win their third Cup in four years.

APRIL 16, 1990

Winnipeg builds a 3-1 series lead over the Oilers in the opening round of the playoffs but fall 4-1 in Edmonton in Game 7. Jets head coach Bob Murdoch, who would be named Coach of the Year after the playoffs, surprises many by starting Stéphane Beauregard over Bob Essensa in the decisive game.

"I'm pretty empty right now," says Dave Ellett. "You're going here, going there, doing this, doing that, and all of a sudden there's nothing. No practice tomorrow, nothing."

JUNE 16, 1990

Unhappy with his ice time and the direction the team is heading, Dale Hawerchuk had asked for a trade at the end of the 1990 season. On this day, he gets his wish as the Jets ship him to the Buffalo Sabres in exchange for Phil Housely, Jeff Parker, Scott Arniel and an exchange of first-round draft picks.

MARCH 2, 1993

A magical night at the Winnipeg Arena as Teemu Selanne, the Finnish Flash, scores three times in a 7-4 loss to the Quebec Nordiques to break Mike Bossy's rookie record of 53 goals. Selanne finishes with 76 that season and 132 points en route to being named the winner of the Calder Trophy as the top rookie.

MAY 6-AUG. 15, 1995

A crazy, emotional roller-coaster ride for the Jets and their fans. It begins on May 6 with a ceremony at the arena known as The Funeral, where the franchise officially retires Thomas Steen's No. 25 and then takes more twists and turns than a California mountain highway. Three days after the ceremony, Operation Grassroots begins as efforts step up to pressure governments to construct a new arena and find local buyers.

On May 16, thousands gather at The Forks and open their piggy banks to the tune of $100,000, and the total ultimately climbs into the millions. Three days after that, Barry Shenkarow reveals the local buyers have missed a deadline and an agreement in principle has been reached with Minneapolis investors. But after a series of broken promises and deadline changes, Shenkarow announces on Aug. 15 the 1995-96 season will be the last for the Jets in Winnipeg.

APRIL 28, 1996

The Jets play their last NHL game, a 4-1 home playoff loss to the Detroit Red Wings. Norm MacIver scores the last Jets goal and the franchise heads to Arizona.

Front-page headline in the *Free Press* the next day: "Born: 1972 Died: 1996 R.I.P. Jets."

"It's like building a cottage from the ground up and enjoying it with your family for years, then returning one year and finding it burned to the ground," said Joe Daley, the Jets' WHA netminder. "I've got a grandson who's five, and he's just getting into the (NHL) game. Now it's over for him."

The NHL YEARS (1979-96)

CHAPTER EIGHT:

Zinger and Kitty

AND now, a love story...

In all his days with the Winnipeg Jets, there was really only one player Craig Heisinger couldn't stand: Randy Carlyle. The fastidious Carlyle was in his sixth season with the Jets when Heisinger arrived in Winnipeg in 1989. He'd been a trainer/equipment manager for the Western Hockey League's Brandon Wheat Kings the previous five seasons.

Carlyle was the unchallenged elder statesman in the Jets' dressing room, and Heisinger was a rookie assistant trainer trying to impress the big-league pros. Especially Carlyle. But nothing worked, and Heisinger came to view Carlyle as a finicky prima donna.

Craig Heisinger, the Winnipeg Jets' new director of player operations, started in pro hockey as the Brandon Wheat Kings' trainer and equipment manager.

Randy Carlyle (left) was the elder statesman when he played for the old Jets. Heisinger, hired as that team's trainer in 1989, couldn't stand him.

WAYNE GLOWACKI WINNIPEG FREE PRESS

Carlyle leads a rush in a game against the Whalers in March 1992. His NHL playing career covered 17 years and more than 1,000 games. He's now the Stanley Cup-winning head coach of the Anaheim Ducks.

"This guy is the biggest jerk on the planet," Heisinger fumed. "He has no time for anybody. He doesn't hang up his gear, he leaves it on a pile on the floor. He moans and bitches about everything. 'Where are the goldfish that go with this water? What's wrong with these sticks? How come they're painted, not dipped?' He could not find a positive in freaking anything. Nothing was ever good enough."

Before one season-opening game in Pittsburgh, Heisinger made the mistake of replacing Carlyle's old underwear — "It was so thin you could see through it." — from his equipment bag with a pair of new, non-transparent ones. Carlyle exploded, "DON'T TOUCH MY GODDAMN UNDERWEAR!!"

"When Randy played, nothing was his fault," Heisinger added. "If he fell down, the trainers couldn't sharpen an axe. If Theo Fleury split his nose open that was my fault because Theo was a friend of mine. During the intermission one night, he grabbed me in the back by the skate sharpener and said, 'You tell that little f--ker if it's the last thing I do, he's dead!' Like it's my fault!"

And so on and so forth.

Years later, pressed on being a jerk and a torment to Heisinger, Carlyle replied matter-of-factly, "I wasn't. He just didn't know what he was doing. He was so inept. I just had to make sure things were done right."

Then came a gorgeous day in Los Angeles, when the young equipment manager was in bliss. The Jets had an off-day on the road, and Heisinger was going to buy a pair of sunglasses and cruise around La La Land in a rented car. Ah, the high life.

But just as Heisinger was leaving the airport, who came along but Carlyle, who walked up and cheerfully inquired, "What are you doing today?"

Heisinger told Carlyle about the sunglasses and the rented car. Carlyle perked up. "Mind if I come along?" he asked.

"I'm thinking, 'Good God, you've got to be kidding me'," Heisinger said. "I've got a day off and I'm going to have to hang with this guy? We never communicated. All he did was yell. But what was I supposed to say?"

KEN GIGLIOTTI WINNIPEG FREE PRESS

Heisinger in June 1999 before moving up from Manitoba Moose trainer into the assistant general manager's job

'He has no time for anybody. He doesn't hang up his gear, he leaves it on a pile on the floor. He moans and bitches about everything. "Where are the goldfish that go with this water? What's wrong with these sticks? How come they're painted, not dipped?" He could not find a positive in freaking anything. Nothing was ever good enough'

Danton Cole (centre) celebrates a goal against Chicago with Troy Murray (right), Carlyle (8) and Phil Housley (rear) in January 1992.

So off the odd couple went to see Hollywood. But Heisinger was still bewildered, even after checking into the Holiday Inn on Redondo Beach and walking across the street to get a piece of Linda's Chocolate Fudge Cake. What was that evil Carlyle up to?

The next day, Carlyle approached Heisinger again, this time asking, "Phil Housley and I are going out to dinner. You want to come?"

To this day, Heisinger isn't really sure what was going on.

"I guess it was like after three years you'd passed this battery of tests and been accepted," Heisinger shrugged. "Maybe it takes other guys longer. It was one of the strangest transformations."

So began one of the closest relationships you'll find in the game and the very foundation of the Manitoba Moose. The Moose franchise was not only instrumental in the development of the hockey careers of Heisinger, Carlyle and owner Mark Chipman, but fundamental to the eventual return of the National Hockey League to Winnipeg years later.

Without the Moose, there would be no Jets, no NHL in Winnipeg. No ownership group of Chipman and Toronto billionaire David Thomson. Randy Carlyle wouldn't have a Stanley Cup ring with the Anaheim Ducks and Heisinger would not be the Winnipeg Jets' director of hockey operations and vice-president of True North Sports & Entertainment.

Yet the genesis of the Moose was a simple matter of Prairie pragmatism: The Jets were leaving in 1996, so the Chipman family decided that the financial commitment they had been prepared to make to the Jets would be invested in acquiring a minor-league team to fill the gaping void. There had to be hockey, right?

Because of his involvement in the Save the Jets campaign, the Chipman clan put Mark in charge of acquiring a team.

The Jets were originally believed to be moving to

The M

I-league ambles into town

By Tim Campbell
Sports Reporter

THE INTERNATIONAL Hockey League returns to Canada for the first time in 32 years this fall and commissioner Bob Ufer says he's not worried in the least about fans with NHL hangovers.

"I don't have that reservation," said Ufer, who was in Winnipeg yesterday for the unveiling of the Manitoba Moose logo and the official announcement that the team has joined the 19-team league.

"I don't want to sound flippant after the NHL hangover, I th_____ ____le are going to be so relie___ ___d the une___

Minneapolis, so logically the Chipmans checked on the availability of the IHL's Minnesota Moose, owned by California-based expat Kevin MacLean. The Moose were struggling, playing in front of empty seats at St. Paul's Civic Center, so a deal to move the team north was quickly brokered.

Suddenly, the young car dealer was the co-owner of a professional hockey franchise, and the learning curve began in earnest.

"I remember it being intense but largely because we were stepping into something we hadn't done before," Chipman said. "It was new to us. It wasn't that we were foreign to running a successful business, it's just that we'd never run a hockey team before. I wouldn't say we were clueless. We were green, for sure, but we weren't running around in the dark."

Chipman became co-owner of the Manitoba Moose after buying the struggling St. Paul, Minn., team from its U.S. owner after the Jets left Winnipeg in 1996. 'We'd never run a hockey team before.'

Winnipeg Free Press

SECTION **C1**

Editor, Julian Rachey / 697-7285

Sports

Thursday, May 2, 1996

ose is loose!

Wesmen women get new coach

U of W passes ball to McKay

By Ashley Prest
Sports Reporter

THE UNIVERSITY of Winnipeg will introduce former all-Canadian Tanya (MacKenzie) McKay today as the new head coach of the University of Winnipeg Wesmen women's basketball team.

So it's a pretty safe bet the team won't be missing too many three-point shots in 1996-97.

After all, McKay was among the top three-point shooters in the country during her five-year career as a Wesmen guard from 1986 to 1991, and in the past five years she has made her mark locally as a coach.

According to sources close to the program, McKay has been hired and recently has been recruiting players for the upcoming season.

U of W athletic director Aubrey Ferris is expected to introduce McKay this afternoon at a press conference at the Duckworth Centre.

"Who's she recruiting for?" Ferris asked yesterday, laughing. "Maybe I should hire her."

The head-coach position was posted in late February but became officially open on April 2 when former head coach Tom Kendall

KEN GIGLIOTTI/WINNIPEG FREE PRESS

Winnipeg Arena.

Wheat Kings' Kevin Cheveldayoff takes a hit from a Seattle Thunderbird.

Cheveldayoff was a hot-shot prospect with the Wheat Kings before being drafted by the New York Islanders in 1988, but a knee injury cut his playing career short.

But if Mark Chipman was the visionary of the operation, and Carlyle the soon-to-be beating heart, undoubtedly the soul of the Moose belonged — and still belongs — to the guy vacuuming the Winnipeg Jets' locker-room in the old Winnipeg Arena that sad April night in 1996.

As a teenager, Craig Heisinger was a backup goaltender for the St. James Canadians whose head probably barely cleared the crossbar. When his playing days ended, however, Heisinger was somewhat adrift when it came to his future. "I didn't want a nine-to-five job like my friends," he said, "but I didn't want to be a gypsy, either."

More than anything, Heisinger loved hockey. He was forever watching the WHA Jets or junior Winnipeg Warriors practise, and one day at the rink it dawned on him that his place in the game might be as a hockey trainer.

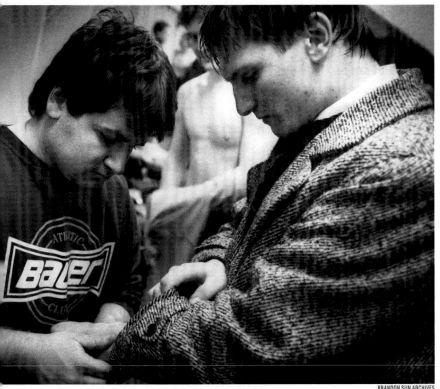
BRANDON SUN ARCHIVES

Heisinger, as Wheat Kings' equipment manager/medical trainer, tends to Jeff Odgers.

Heisinger proudly announced his intentions to his parents Vic and Kay, whose reaction was a mixture of confusion and horror. Vic had encouraged his son to pursue a career in aviation mechanics, but after a brief fling as an apprentice Heisinger quickly concluded, "I couldn't fix a lawn mower, much less an airplane."

The 22-year-old Heisinger eventually landed a job with the Wheat Kings and in 1984 set off for Brandon driving a Ford Courier pickup truck loaded with his worldly possessions, some clothes, a sewing machine and a yellow dresser.

In the Wheat City, he lived in a trailer park behind a McDonald's, just off the Trans-Canada Highway.

Heisinger was the Wheat Kings' equipment manager and medical trainer, although he had no medical training. "You read a book on how to tape a hamstring," he explained, "and that's what you did."

Heisinger's first lesson: What can go wrong will go wrong. Once, a Wheaties goalie had his leg cut open by a skate blade. When Heisinger rushed to the player's side and rolled him over, the exposed artery started shooting blood everywhere. "It was like wrestling," he said, but the "medical trainer" didn't panic and stemmed the bleeding.

Heisinger was determined. He read more books on tending to injuries. He became a specialist at repairing skates and gloves with the $1,500 sewing machine he'd purchased a few years before. For Heisinger, the Wheat Kings were Hockey U. (It was in Brandon that Heisinger also first crossed paths with a 15-year-old defenceman named Kevin Cheveldayoff, a hot-shot Wheat Kings prospect. "He was a kid you didn't forget," Heisinger remembered. But more on that later.)

As Heisinger's reputation grew, he served as trainer for Team Canada's world junior squad at the 1988 championships in Moscow. When Heisinger returned to Canada, the Jets were calling. John Ferguson offered him a job with the AHL's Moncton Hawks, the Jets' farm team. Heisinger turned Fergie down, and the intimidating GM was taken aback.

"That could hurt your chances of getting back to Winnipeg," Ferguson warned.

"It might," a confident Heisinger replied, "but at the end of the day when you have to replace somebody here you're still going to hire the best guy. And I'm the best guy."

Honesty was a trait Ferguson always admired. Heisinger joined the Jets in the fall of 1989.

But it wasn't until the Jets' demise in 1996 that Heisinger, Chipman and Carlyle found themselves on the same team. Even before Chipman bought the IHL's Moose, he was told Heisinger would be a necessity. The worst-kept secret in professional sports is that good trainers are worth their weight in gold.

In fact, before the Jets vanished into the Arizona desert, Heisinger had agreed to stay behind and join the Moose. Meanwhile, Carlyle interviewed for the position of head coach and GM, but was passed over for the better-known Jean Perron, who had won a Stanley Cup behind the bench of the Montreal

'You read a book on how to tape a hamstring, and that's what you did'

Jean Perron, first coach of the Moose, and Randy Carlyle share views at practice in September 1996.

Canadiens in 1985-86.

Carlyle was hired as assistant coach and assistant GM.

Before joining the Moose, Perron had been at the helm of the IHL's San Francisco Spiders, which had folded. "I think it's going to be much more interesting in Winnipeg," Perron ventured, when introduced to the Winnipeg media.

Alas, truer words have rarely been spoken. As rookie mistakes for a fledgling franchise go, hiring Perron would rank up there with putting the captain of the Exxon Valdez behind the wheel.

After all, the inaugural Manitoba Moose in 1996-97 had enough strikes against them trying to fill the NHL void with a minor-league outfit that, for many Jets fans, was just salt in an open wound. It was like replacing the Rolling Stones with the Archies — even if the Stones never really won anything, anyway.

It's not just that the Moose stumbled out of the gate, with the only recognizable name being homegrown Randy Gilhen, a former Jet and Manitoba's first team captain. Worse, it soon became evident the Moose had no discernible system. Cracks began to surface in the dressing room and the tightly wound Perron was railing every other day in the papers, threatening to make wholesale changes.

By early February 1997, the Moose were dead last in their division with a 16-26-8 record. But the final straw came when Perron cut Manitoba forward Scott Allison at 6 a.m. in an airport in Kalamazoo, of all places.

Chipman fired Perron a couple of days later.

Then it got ugly. Perron threatened legal action against the Moose and claimed captain Gilhen had back-stabbed him with the players. Perron suggested Carlyle was plotting against him, too.

Other than that, everything was just peachy.

If the Moose were a sink-or-swim proposition, the sharks were swirling. In fact, it would take years for the Moose to overcome the unfortunate gong show of Year One in Winnipeg, at least for local hockey fans who already turned up their noses at the IHL brand.

"The real tough part for us was that you only get one chance to make a first impression," Gilhen said, "and our first impression wasn't good."

Randy Carlyle

Randy Gilhen

John Ferguson

The "Jets Mafia" enjoy a few laughs at a November 2005 get-together at the Winnipeg Arena.

Randy Carlyle

But the turmoil sowed the seeds for a future none of the participants could envision.

In early February 1997, Mark Chipman promoted Carlyle to head coach of the yearling Moose.

Carlyle was a born leader who came to adore John Ferguson from their early days with the Jets, when the GM invited the defenceman to plop down 10 large to buy a pony named Clear Choice. Somebody cracked to Carlyle: "Once you cut the horns off that thing, it might have a chance." Clear Choice never made it to the races.

But Ferguson and Carlyle would become lifelong friends and allies. (Years later, when Carlyle was GM of the Moose, Ferguson was hospitalized for an emergency angioplasty to deal with a racing heartbeat. Ferguson didn't want Carlyle to read about the minor surgery in the paper, so he called his friend Ted Foreman in Winnipeg to relay the information to the Moose boss. As luck would have it, Carlyle was in Montreal at the time and rushed straight to the hospital and within minutes arrived at Ferguson's room. Fergie looked at Carlyle and deadpanned, "What took you so long?")

"He was gruff and wanted to be an intimidating force and he was," Carlyle said of his mentor. "But he had another side that a lot of people didn't get to see. I got to see that right away."

What did Carlyle learn from Ferguson?

"The intensity level that he committed toward the game was second to none," Carlyle said. "And I think at times it was a positive and at times it was a negative for him. He was loyal to a fault and he was intense to a fault. But he was a great human being. He wanted nothing more than to win and he would do anything he could to win. He would stand by his player through thick and thin. He would take on all comers, and you knew that."

Funny, but if you ask former Jet Thomas Steen to describe Carlyle, the answer is eerily similar. "He was all heart," Steen noted. "He had passion, like Fergie. Competitive like crazy. He didn't really have top-notch skills but he overcame that with passion and competitiveness. And he was a great team guy. Always with the one-liners. He kept everybody sharp."

there is some unintentional-yet-ironic relevance.)

Before Perron was fired, it was clear he'd lost some of the players' respect. In fact, every time the head coach entered the dressing room, one veteran would bark "security" just loud enough for the others to hear. As in, someone call security because there's a mad man on the loose. But Perron was oblivious to the inside joke. Regardless of what he thought of Perron, Carlyle bristled at the blatant show of disrespect.

During his first day as head coach, Carlyle gathered the team in the dressing room and laid down his laws. There would be systems installed offensively and defensively. There would be respect for the team and the game. There would be discipline. Above all, there would be an unquestioned boss who held each of them accountable.

"And one more thing," Carlyle added, before he left the room on Day One. "If I hear f--king 'security' once in this f--king dressing room again, get the f--k out of here. Just take your f--king bags and go!"

The Moose rallied to finish 16-14 down the stretch and just fell short of a playoff berth. Over the next 14 years, the franchise would miss qualifying for the post-season only once.

The word "security" was never uttered in the Manitoba Moose dressing room again.

Indeed, if security was ever required, it would have been when Heisinger and Carlyle, the Bickersons of hockey, were embroiled in one of their frequent spats.

One night, midway through the 1997-98 season, the Moose were in Detroit playing the Vipers. It was the end of a dismal seven-game road trip in which the Moose would win just twice. The Moose power play was oh-fer-everything.

"Randy was coaching," Heisinger said. "At least, he was TRYING to coach."

Sure enough, on his first shift of the game, Moose forward Rhett Gordon blew a tire and hit the ice. Heisinger could feel Carlyle's eyes burning in the back of his head. If a player falls, it's the trainer's fault, according to the Book of Carlyle. Then Gordon falls down again.

BORIS MINKEVICH WINNIPEG FREE PRESS

"Kitty" Carlyle, in his Winnipeg Arena office in August 1997 — a take-charge guy and intense competitor.

And Steen mildly disagrees that Carlyle's take-charge style was gleaned from Ferguson. It was already evident in Pittsburgh, where Carlyle was a top defenceman. Steen cited the trade that brought Carlyle to the Jets. "They really went after Randy," Steen said. "Out of all the guys in the NHL, they wanted Randy Carlyle. Fergie saw that (leadership) in him and that's the guy he wanted. He had it already."

Chipman recognized the same traits, making the hard decision to fire Perron much more palatable.

"I had a real level of comfort from that moment on," Chipman said. "As soon as Kitty took over, I felt that the team was in the hands of a professional."

(Author's note: Kitty is Carlyle's nickname, perhaps one of the most inaccurate handles in professional hockey history. However, since the biggest claim to fame of legendary American singer and actress Kitty Carlisle, the source of Carlyle's moniker, was her stardom as a panellist on the 1950s game show, *To Tell the Truth*,

There would be systems installed offensively and defensively. There would be respect for the team and the game. There would be discipline. Above all, there would be an unquestioned boss who held each of them accountable

Moose forward Rhett Gordon hits the ice as he tries to keep control of the puck against the Kansas City Blades in December 1998.

Boom goes the dynamite. The game was still going when Carlyle "went nuts" on his equipment manager, who knew the explosion was coming. Two recently acquired players, goaltender Johan Hedberg and forward Scott Thomas, sat in stunned silence as Carlyle ripped into Heisinger. The odd expletive was uttered.

Heisinger took the tirade and then fired back at Carlyle, "I'm so sick and tired of your shit! We're 2-5 on this trip. Why don't you sharpen the f--king skates and I'll run the bench!"

Indeed, the complex dynamics between Heisinger and Carlyle would keep Sigmund Freud scribbling notes until his fingers were numb. Chipman described the pair's relationship as so "incredibly deep" that it can "endure their respective personalities."

"They have, since the beginning, been very frank with one another," he noted. "And it's probably only strengthened their friendship."

Like the time in the mid-'90s, shortly after Carlyle had retired with over 1,000 NHL games played in an accomplished 17-year career, and the two were driving back to Winnipeg from a fishing trip to Lake of the Woods. Carlyle was lamenting his inability to find a hockey job. The only position he could find was the colour guy for local radio, which was a problem because Carlyle despised the media on principle.

Carlyle just wanted an opportunity to prove himself as a coach. He'd had a handshake agreement with Winnipeg ownership for a job in some capacity behind the Jets' bench after he retired in 1993, but Mike Smith couldn't or wouldn't find a place for Carlyle.

Heisinger didn't know that, but he'd had enough. "Stop whining," he said. "You've got to start over. Those 1,000 games you played, they don't mean a thing anymore."

The pep talk didn't go over well.

"What do you mean those games don't matter?!" Carlyle yelled at his best friend. "What have you ever done?!"

For the next two hours, Carlyle didn't say a word. He sat in the car, seething. Heisinger didn't hear from him for three weeks.

A decade later, Randy Carlyle would lead the Anaheim Ducks to a Stanley Cup. And no one on the planet would have been prouder than Heisinger. But in the beginning, there was an unbreakable bond formed between two bullheaded personalities who valued honesty above all else.

"To me, those things... all I've ever said to people was that I wanted to be told the truth," Carlyle reasoned, when reminded of the tense fishing excursion. "If I can't handle the truth then it's my fault."

Chipman agreed that the relationships formed among him, Carlyle and Heisinger were critical to the franchise's formative years. After all, heated disagreements are not uncommon among passionate, competitive individuals.

Case in point: Heisinger and future Moose head coach Alain Vigneault would often knock heads like rutting rams. They had one particularly heated screaming match in the lobby of a hotel in Grand Rapids after a playoff game. The pair yelled at each other as they got on the elevator, then rode up in stony silence. The door opened, they stepped out and Vigneault said, "Breakfast tomorrow morning?"

"It results in harsh words," Chipman said, "but never hurt feelings. One of the things that bonds us together is that type of honesty. It's not for the faint of heart."

The Moose managed to survive their inauspicious debut. Carlyle, the head coach and GM, signed players and coached. But Heisinger was the team's Radar O'Reilly not just serving as equipment manager and resident fixer, but making sure all the paperwork was filed with league headquarters.

"That's where I really needed the help and that's where Craig Heisinger was the MVP," Carlyle said. "Because I could do all of the coaching and player acquisition and the contracts and Zinger was the guy who made sure all the I's and T's were dotted and crossed. He did that as the equipment manager and I knew he could do it in management. His talent was being wasted. And that's not said in a negative way to people who do that job. It's just there was so much more for him to do, because if you ever gave Zinger a task, he didn't complain, he just got it done. He finds a way."

Head coach Alain Vigneault watches a Moose inter-squad practice at the MTS Centre in September 2005. He and GM Heisinger butted heads a few times.

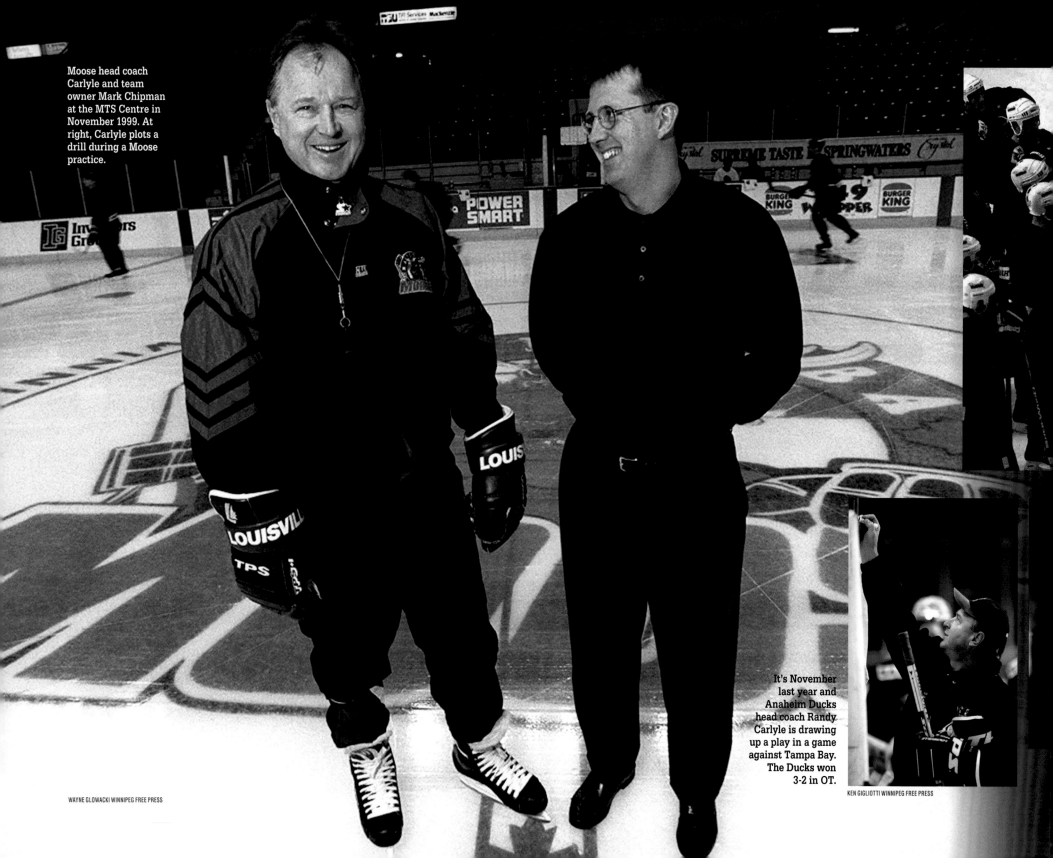

Moose head coach Carlyle and team owner Mark Chipman at the MTS Centre in November 1999. At right, Carlyle plots a drill during a Moose practice.

It's November last year and Anaheim Ducks head coach Randy Carlyle is drawing up a play in a game against Tampa Bay. The Ducks won 3-2 in OT.

WAYNE GLOWACKI WINNIPEG FREE PRESS

KEN GIGLIOTTI WINNIPEG FREE PRESS

Carlyle

In 1999, Carlyle finally persuaded a reluctant Heisinger to leave his sewing machine behind and become a full-time assistant GM. By the 2000-01 season, Carlyle and Heisinger had built an IHL contender that appeared primed to take a serious run at the Turner Cup. But in February, the Moose lost four key players to the NHL: Scott Thomas (Los Angeles), goaltender Johan Hedberg (Pittsburgh), defenceman Philippe Boucher (Los Angeles) and veteran John MacLean (Dallas).

The decimated Moose eventually lost to the Chicago Wolves — Manitoba's version of the Jets' nemesis Edmonton Oilers — in the second round of the IHL playoffs. But for the first time since the Jets had departed, the Moose had generated a genuine ripple of playoff interest.

"That's something that hadn't occurred in this city," Chipman said. "It may not have resonated with a lot of people, but to me that was big. I was thinking, 'Wow, we've got something here. We've built something.' Those early years with the Moose, that's when we really learned to run a team."

The following season, the Moose landscape would undergo a dramatic change with the folding of the IHL into the American Hockey League and Manitoba's subsequent affiliation with the NHL's Vancouver Canucks.

No longer were the Moose an independent organization, and suddenly the tight-knit Original Three were taking their marching orders from Vancouver. It wasn't a seamless transition, given the Canucks' farm system had for years been an unkempt outfit known as the Syracuse Crunch, which had produced little in the way of victories or prospects for the big club.

Not surprisingly, Carlyle left to assume an assistant coaching position with the Washington Capitals in 2002-03. That same year, Moose assistant coach Scott Arniel, another former Jets player who had been mentoring under Carlyle, bolted for a similar job with the Buffalo Sabres.

Chipman asked Heisinger to assume the job as Moose GM. But the former trainer was hesitant. "What would the hockey world think?"

After all, Heisinger was always self-conscious about his humble beginnings, at least when it came to the perception of entering upper management. But Heisinger also believed strongly his roots in the bowels of the dressing room were invaluable in running a club from the top down. "I would never discount that. Never," he said. "I can't fall back on what I didn't do. I have to fall back on what I did do."

Once he took the position, there was no turning back. Heisinger, left to fend on his own without Carlyle or Arniel, soon realized — like his days as a medical trainer with no medical training — the only way to succeed was to push forward. And when necessary, to push back.

Not long into the Moose-Canucks partnership, all was not well down on the farm. The Moose had always put a premium on winning, and Heisinger wasn't convinced the Canucks were paying enough attention to the lacklustre performance of their middle-of-the-road AHL club.

The Manitoba GM was in a slow burn.

Finally, Heisinger persuaded then-Vancouver GM Brian Burke to meet in Utah, where the Moose had a two-game set with the Grizzlies. The Moose stank up the place, which Heisinger thought would only help his argument.

After the second game, Burke and Heisinger met just outside the Moose dressing room, where the Canucks' GM — himself an opinionated, forceful Irishman — began to defend the team. Heisinger just heard excuses.

So a choice had to be made right there in Utah. "Either I accept this and shut up," Heisinger thought, "or stand up for myself that this isn't acceptable."

Of course, given Heisinger's nature, there was really no choice at all. The Moose GM got into Burke's belly button. Recalled Heisinger: "I went up one side of him and down the other. And as I was coming down I could see he was really getting hot. I thought I'd better cut this off."

Too late. Burke was smoking. Furious, he stooped down to pick up his bag, stood up and peered down at Heisinger. "Who the hell are you to talk to me like that, you little f--king Eskimo!" Burke bellowed.

"I'm nobody," Heisinger replied, "but that's what I think."

Burke stormed off, back to Vancouver. Heisinger returned to Winnipeg.

It was a defining moment in Heisinger's career, that he had the fortitude, right or wrong, to stand up for his beliefs — even when it came to challenging a seasoned, respected NHL executive such as Burke.

Except in all the commotion, Heisinger forgot one thing: Two weeks later, Burke was scheduled to speak at the Sportsman's Dinner in Brandon — and Heisinger was supposed to introduce him.

When the time came, Heisinger picked Burke up at the Winnipeg airport. You could hear crickets. Finally, with a two-hour drive to Brandon ahead, Burke turned to Heisinger and said, "What do you say we both turn off our phones and talk this out?"

They did. And the Canucks-Moose relationship prospered.

In 2004-05, Carlyle returned to coach the Moose — this time with his old trainer now serving as his boss — and led the Moose

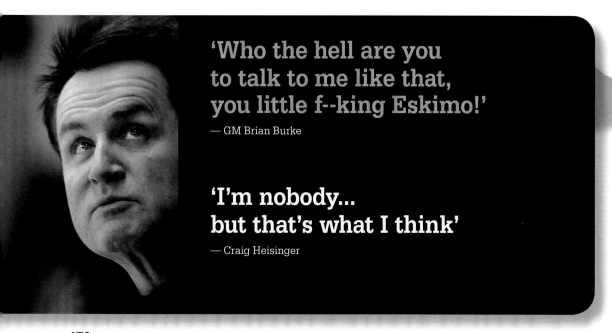

'Who the hell are you to talk to me like that, you little f--king Eskimo!'
— GM Brian Burke

'I'm nobody... but that's what I think'
— Craig Heisinger

to a 44-win season, which included a playoff run to the Calder Cup semifinal.

The next season, Carlyle was hired as the head coach of the Ducks — by Burke, who had left the Canucks after the 2003-04 season. Together, they won the Cup in 2007.

Meanwhile, Alain Vigneault coached the Moose in 2005-06, before being promoted to Vancouver and replaced in Manitoba by Arniel, a Carlyle disciple.

In Arniel's four seasons in Manitoba, the Moose set season records for wins (50) and points (107) in 2008-09, and advanced to the Calder Cup final for the first and only time in franchise history, before succumbing to the Hershey Bears 4-2.

For five seasons (2005-10), the Moose were led by captain and three-time Stanley Cup champion Mike Keane, a proud son of Winnipeg who embodied the traditional hockey principles Chipman, Heisinger and Carlyle — like Ferguson before them — had demanded.

"We had our scrapes along the way, but we made it work," Chipman said. "We had something like 13 or 14 playoff series wins (13, in fact, compared to the Jets' two.) "No matter what the challenges we had along the way, we built a team that was competitive. We were never a joke as a team."

By 2010-2011, the Moose were drawing more than 8,000 fans a game to the MTS Centre, a modest yet state-of-the-art arena (seating capacity 15,015) that opened in November 2004. The franchise was the gold standard of the American Hockey League.

Chipman was named the AHL's Executive of the Year in 2005. Heisinger received the same award in 2009.

In all, Heisinger's teams missed the playoffs only once in his nine years as Moose GM, when Manitoba's overall record was 381-254-35-50. No one was wondering what the hockey world would think of Craig Heisinger anymore.

Except, perhaps, for one person: Craig Heisinger, who despite his AHL success balked at Chipman's offer to be GM of the NHL club.

"Everything he's done, every step he's taken, he's thought about," Chipman said. "He's not an impetuous guy. His biggest concern has always been — I don't want to say self-doubt — but

TREVOR HAGAN WINNIPEG FREE PRES

Three-time Stanley Cup winner Mike Keane wore the C as he led the Moose for five seasons from 2005 to 2010.

Under head coach Scott Arniel, the Moose in 2008-09 set season records for wins and points and went to the AHL Calder Cup championship for the first time.

because he came from (the equipment room)... he's always had this fear no one would take him seriously. A huge fear. That's part of the reason he's worked so hard; not to prove to other people but to prove to himself he's deserving of the opportunities.

"I've worked with the guy for 15 years. I'd walk over broken glass for him."

Heisinger eventually accepted the role of Jets director of player operations simply because that's his forte; stay ensconced in the background, fix problems and scout and sign players. That's the most comfortable suit in the closet of a man who, if he had the power, would make cargo shorts part of the NHL's mandatory dress code.

So the band still plays on, in a way.

"Carlyle and Zinger were the model to me," Chipman said, of the trio's Moose journey. "It was their lead that I followed. We made it our own. And those guys became fiercely proud of what we were doing. Zinger more so than anybody. The Moose became more part of his DNA than the Jets were, because it's the environment where he went from being a highly regarded equipment trainer to a bona fide NHL executive. If it was up to him, that's what the (NHL) team would be called."

It's true. On the day the NHL returned to Winnipeg, Heisinger took his turn at the podium during the press conference thinking his little speech would be a breeze. Then just as he got to the part about thanking the Moose faithful, the waterworks started coming.

Yes, the irascible old skate sharpener started to weep.

"I thought the role the Manitoba Moose played in bringing the NHL back kinda got lost," Heisinger explained. "It's not because there's a faction of people out there that decided not to come to a game for 15 years and waited patiently for the NHL to come back. It's because of the loyal base of Moose fans that let a lot of guys who were just cutting their teeth in professional hockey at a variety of levels — a coach, a player or an equipment guy — make mistakes. Those people were patient with us and gave us a chance to move on to bigger and better things."

Heisinger prepares to announce Claude Noel as the sixth head coach of the Manitoba Moose in June last year.

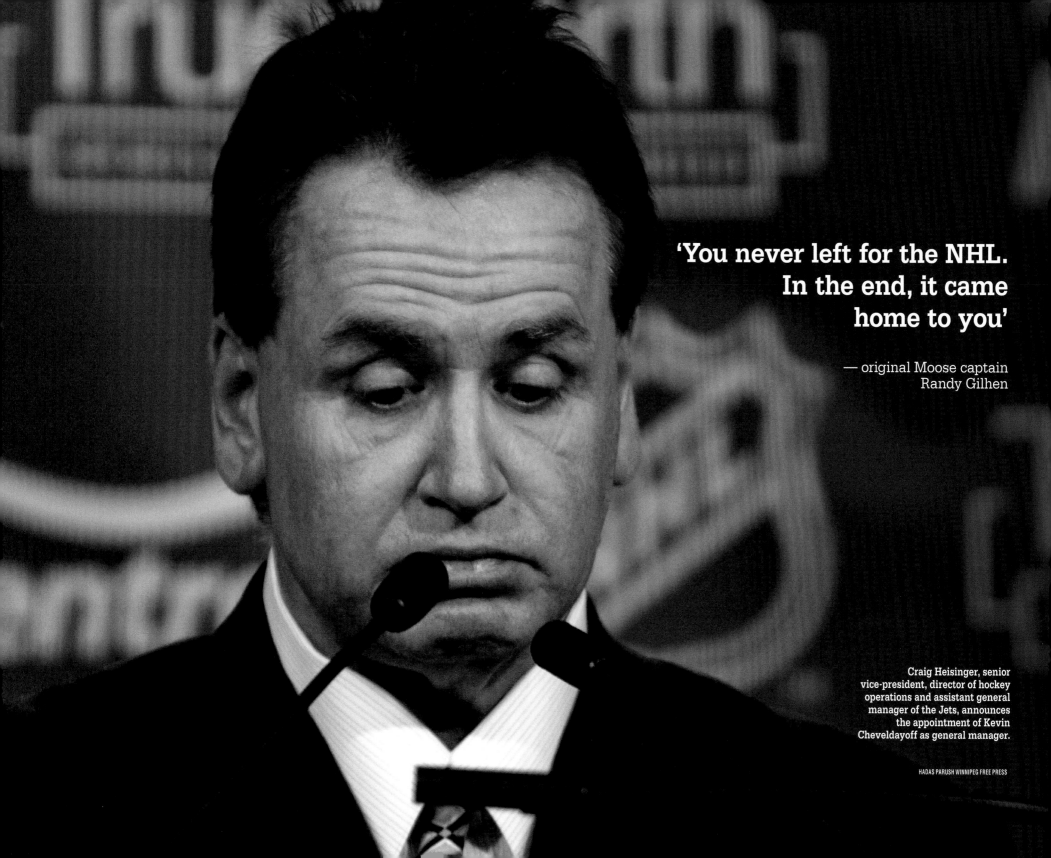

'You never left for the NHL.
In the end, it came
home to you'

— original Moose captain
Randy Gilhen

Craig Heisinger, senior
vice-president, director of hockey
operations and assistant general
manager of the Jets, announces
the appointment of Kevin
Cheveldayoff as general manager.

"It wasn't just me; it was Randy, it was Arnie, it was all kinds of people. (Moose favourite) Jimmy Roy. And I didn't want that to get lost in the translation. I thought that would be simple to say. Apparently it was not.

"There was a lot of blood, sweat and tears put in," Heisinger added. "But Mark wouldn't be as good an owner without the Manitoba Moose. I wouldn't have had what I have. Randy Carlyle wouldn't be coach of the Stanley Cup-winning Anaheim Ducks. People lose sight of that. The Vancouver Canucks wouldn't be in the Stanley Cup final (in 2011) without the Manitoba Moose. That's just fact.

"The role the Manitoba Moose has played in Manitoba hockey history with the NHL coming back and probably not going anywhere ever again... for me, it was 15 years of my life. I couldn't let that go. It's not easy to move past that."

It was an emotional time not lost on those who were with the Moose from the beginning. Remember, Heisinger never chased the NHL to Phoenix. He stayed in Winnipeg, his hometown, to raise his children and a hockey franchise.

Somewhere along the way, the Moose became his family, too.

Indeed, if hockey has fairy tales, Heisinger is as close as you can get to Cinderella, even if the visual image would be unsettling. He agrees: "It's an unlikely story," Heisinger acknowledged. "But it usually happens to somebody else."

When the NHL returned, Heisinger got a text message from original Moose captain Randy Gilhen that, in effect, read, "You never left for the NHL. In the end, it came home to you."

So it was that a man as crusty as week-old pumpernickel cried the day the NHL left Winnipeg, and he cried when it came back, too.

But Craig Heisinger's tears weren't meant for the Jets the second time around, you see.

They were for the Manitoba Moose.

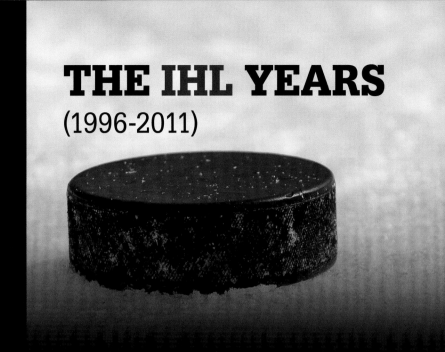

THE IHL YEARS
(1996-2011)

▶ OCT. 4, 1996

The Manitoba Moose — formerly the Minnesota Moose — make their International Hockey League debut with a 4-3 shootout road loss to the Milwaukee Admirals. Former Montreal Canadiens head coach Jean Perron is the first bench boss, but is replaced by Randy Carlyle after a 16-26-8 start. Even though the club plays over .500 under Carlyle, they miss the playoffs in their first IHL season with a 32-40-10 record.

▶ OCT. 5, 2001

After Moose leave the IHL to join the AHL — and officially become the Vancouver Canucks' affiliate — and with Canucks legend Stan Smyl as head coach — Manitoba loses its first game in the new circuit 3-1 to the Saint John Flames in New Brunswick.

▶ NOV. 6, 2004

The Moose bid adieu — to the Winnipeg Arena with a 2-1 shootout loss to the Utah Grizzlies in front of 13,985. Former Jets Norm Beaudin, Peter

Sullivan and Bill Lesuk are there as is Teemu Selanne. "There was lots of warm and fuzzy feelings and a lot of memories relived," says Moose general manager Craig Heisinger. "It's a special place here. To watch this go away, it's not going to be easy for me."

And 10 days later the $133.5-million 15,015-seat MTS Centre opens in downtown Winnipeg.

▶ MARCH 26, 2006

The Winnipeg Arena —which opened in 1955 to replace the old Amphitheatre, is officially demolished.

▶ JUNE 12, 2009

The Moose post a league-best — 50-23-1-6 mark and Scott Arniel is named the AHL's top coach. But the season ends on a sour note with the club losing the Calder Cup final in six games to the Hershey Bears with a 4-2 loss in front of a crowd of 15,003 at the MTS Centre.

"They're a good team, give them credit," says Moose forward Jason Krog. "But it sucks to lose this way."

MTS centre

MTS

Mark Chipman

CHAPTER NINE:

Chipman in Charge

THE scene: It's the early 1990s and the Toronto Maple Leafs are in Winnipeg to play the Jets. As usual, you can't judge by the assembled crowd at the Winnipeg Arena which is the home team.

That Leaf-loving sentiment stuck in the craw of one particular Jets diehard, who just happened to find himself, along with a childhood friend, passing by the visiting dressing room during an intermission. Out stepped Toronto head coach Pat Burns with one of his assistants for a little fresh air.

The grand opening of the MTS Centre on Nov. 16, 2004 featured performances by Burton Cummings, Randy Bachman, Chantal Kreviazuk, Doc Walker, Tom Cochrane and the Winnipeg Symphony Orchestra.

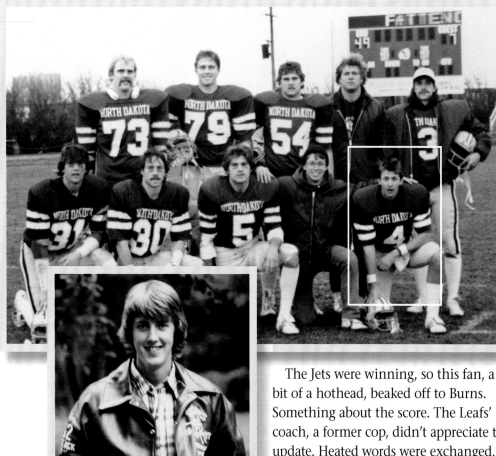

PHOTO S COURTESY OF CHIPMAN FAMILY

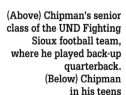

(Above) Chipman's senior class of the UND Fighting Sioux football team, where he played back-up quarterback. (Below) Chipman in his teens

The Jets were winning, so this fan, a bit of a hothead, beaked off to Burns. Something about the score. The Leafs' coach, a former cop, didn't appreciate the update. Heated words were exchanged. Tempers flared. Next thing you know, the head of NHL security at the arena, another former cop named Bob Martell, appeared and grabbed the Jets troublemaker and his buddy by their collars.

"What the hell are you guys doing here?!" Martell demanded, while escorting the civilian instigators out of the restricted area. "Get the f--k out!!"

Ladies and gentleman, meet the future owner of the Winnipeg Jets, Mark Chipman, and the president and CEO of True North Sports & Entertainment, Jim Ludlow.

"Aw, crap," Chipman sighed, when the incident was broached. "I'm not talking about that. That should not be part of this story."

Too late, Mark. So what happened?

The owner of the Winnipeg Jets confessed.

"I said something to Burns about the score of the game," he began. "I was not a Leafs fan. It used to drive me nuts that there were as many Leafs fans in the building as Jets fans. I'm not exaggerating, right? I mean, you couldn't tell who scored and that really used to get me fired up.

"Anyway, that wasn't the end of the conversation (with Burns and the assistant). The next thing you know, Bob (Martell) was there. We got sort of ushered away. Let's just say it was an intense conversation for a couple of seconds."

Chipman and Ludlow were in their early 30s at the time. They'd known each other dating back to minor-hockey days in their early teens. Chipman was a defenceman from St. James. Ludlow was a forward for Assiniboine Park. Both of them strived to make their respective AA teams. Said Ludlow: "We were sort of the guys who were the last cut every year."

Until they were 16 and both reached their modest minor-hockey goals.

Chipman and Ludlow enrolled in St. Paul's High School in 1974. But they hung out together mostly during the summer in Gimli, where Ludlow's parents had a cottage. By day, they ran their respective "small businesses;" Ludlow's house-painting operation consisted of a truck and a ladder, Chipman's lawn-care venture was a truck and a mower.

Ludlow's painting business helped pay for law school at Osgoode Hall in Toronto. Chipman, meanwhile, went on to attend the University of North Dakota, where he served as backup quarterback for the Fighting Sioux in what could charitably be described as an uneventful athletic career.

More importantly, Chipman graduated UND with an honours BA in economics and juris doctorate in law. And he met his future wife, Patti.

Ludlow eventually returned to Winnipeg and joined the law firm of Aikins, MacAuley & Thorvaldson. Chipman and Patti moved to Florida, where he set up shop as a district attorney in the mid-1980s. "Nothing really glamorous," he said.

Chipman and Ludlow remained in touch, of course, but clearly their fledgling careers had met a fork in the road. Their days of banding together to express their mutual disdain for the Toronto Maple Leafs were over.

Everything changed, however, in 1988 when Chipman returned to Winnipeg and took up his father Bob's offer to help run the family auto business. By 1992, Chipman was president of the Birchwood Automotive Group.

"I felt like I needed to do something on my own," Chipman noted. "But it's the best decision I ever made, moving back to Winnipeg and working for my father."

Chipman was no longer in the lawn-cutting business. Ludlow had stowed his ladder. And soon their worlds began to intersect again. Ludlow's firm was involved in the sale of the Winnipeg Jets to Burke and Gluckstern. So Chipman recruited his old buddy to broker the sale of the Minnesota Moose to Manitoba.

In fact, from the beginning of the Moose, Chipman tried to convince Ludlow of the previously impossible: to construct a new downtown arena that could be built with mostly private financing and serve as a centrepiece for a self-sustaining sports and entertainment enterprise.

It's just that Chipman had only one piece of the puzzle, a no-name IHL team playing in an antiquated, revenue-starved arena.

Ludlow was skeptical.

"Come on," he said. "That's like starting with a used car lot and building an empire."

Interesting analogy. After all, back in 1960, Robert Chipman had moved back to Winnipeg after 10 years out in southern Ontario working for a lending firm called the Industrial Acceptance Corporation, which provided loans for post-war purchases such as automobiles, heavy equipment and appliances.

The corporation wanted Chipman to move back out east, but he was just starting a young family with his wife, Sheila, and was determined to stay in his hometown. In his own words, the elder Chipman was "working hard and not making very much money."

Chipman didn't want to leave. His family's roots in Winnipeg were deep. His mother Natalie's grandfather (last name Houde) was an acquaintance of Louis Riel. "We go back a long way in this city," he said.

So Robert Chipman resigned from his job at IAC, cashed in his meagre pension and opened a small used car lot on Portage Avenue with a tiny mobile hut that served as an office. In essence, the elder Chipman started with squat, hope and a bunch of 1950s Chevs and Pontiacs.

In 1963, Chipman was approached to run a GM dealership at the corner of Portage Avenue and Moray Street called Birchwood Motors. Within five years, Birchwood was one of the top five dealerships in Winnipeg.

The family business model emerged: Revenues from existing businesses were reinvested back into new business and expansion.

One dealership grew to five, to 10, to 15. Chipman formed a real estate company, then a company called National Leasing, in the model of IAC.

By the mid-2000s, the annual revenue from the Chipmans' joint ventures had reached north of $420 million. National Leasing alone was valued at $130 million when it was sold to the Canadian Western Bank in 2009 — but only after the CWB agreed to keep the company's head office in Winnipeg, a stipulation Robert made himself.

Apparently, building an empire from a used car lot was not inconceivable to the Chipmans — neither in the 1960s nor three decades later — when son Mark began to notice that state-of-the-art downtown arenas in places like Cleveland (Quicken) and Grand Rapids (Van Andel) — two Moose rivals — were proof that the privately led construction of a Winnipeg model was feasible.

Forget the long-festering opposition to a new Winnipeg Arena, a concept that had been repeatedly floated, analyzed and ultimately shelved for almost three decades. Said Chipman: "Toxic environment notwithstanding, it seemed like a topic worth exploring."

So it was at the turn of the century that Ludlow agreed to become Employee No. 1 of True North Sports & Entertainment.

Also in 1999, the embryonic True North found an ally in then-newly elected Manitoba premier Gary Doer. At the same time, then-Winnipeg mayor Glen Murray was pursuing any projects that could help rejuvenate a deteriorating core, especially along a fading Portage Avenue.

The Eaton's department store — once the jewel of the city's downtown that symbolized the city's prosperity for the first half of the 20th century — was an abandoned, decaying hulk. The building where Winnipeggers spent 50 cents of every dollar from 1905 until the 1960s was now full of pigeon droppings.

"What did that say about this city's dynamism and ability to move forward? Not a lot," Ludlow said. "And it wasn't just a reflection of what people in Winnipeg thought, but how people outside of Winnipeg thought. They were thinking, 'What's happened to Winnipeg?'

"That might have been the bottom. The city had really bogged down. If you look through the '90s, the slow decay of the downtown of the city, it weighed heavily on a lot of people. The city can't afford to keep the team. It's going to a big, fancy place in the desert called Phoenix. There's the odd tumbleweed blowing by. OK, maybe we should just accept who we are, not who we thought we were at one point in time. Let's be complacent to be in the middle. Let's be satisfied with mediocrity. It created an attitude of, 'Let's move somewhere else.'"

You know, like the Winnipeg Jets.

But Chipman wasn't going anywhere. He'd been raised in a family where his father's motto was always, "The winners in this world are those that give."

If that sounds hokey to the cynical, it never did to the son. "He is a rare combination of so many wonderful qualities," Mark said of his father. "He's one of the most humble guys I've ever known. He's had a great deal of success and always done it with humility."

It was that philosophy (or philanthropy) that spawned the Moose. But don't think for a second that the arena, for Chipman, was about anything but business and profit from the very beginning.

At first, Chipman's notion was to build south of Portage, neighbouring the city's convention centre. Once again, however, fate would intervene. As Chipman was formulating his arena venture, a Toronto-based company called Osmington Inc. had acquired the assets of a Dutch pension fund. Those included the Eaton's property in Winnipeg.

As such, Osmington had just inherited a dilapidated property along a devaluating piece of downtown real estate in a city engulfed in an economic funk. Good luck.

Enter mayor Murray, who became a matchmaker of sorts, inviting Osmington CEO George Schott on a tour of Grand Rapids' Van Andel Arena, with a delegation that included Ludlow and Chipman. The boys from Winnipeg had no idea why the "grey-haired fellow" from Toronto was on the trip. They didn't know the first thing about Osmington Inc., either.

Eaton's Winnipeg downtown store was demolished to make room for the MTS Centre.

EATON'S

EATONS

EATON'S

Ex-Winnipeg mayor Glen Murray

WAYNE GLOWACKI WINNIPEG FREE PRES

The grey-haired fellow was Schott. And his boss was David Kenneth Roy Thomson, 3rd Baron Thomson of Fleet, the richest man in Canada and, according to *Forbes*, the 17th-richest man in the world with an estimated worth of $23 billion.

"It was a total coincidence," Ludlow allowed. "Today, you can call that serendipity. At the time it was called, 'Hey, I've got a piece of real estate that's worthless to me. Maybe it will work with your project. Maybe you should come to Portage Avenue.'"

Was this just blind luck? Or maybe it was a city that had taken some knocks and was finally, as they like to say in sports, getting the bounces.

Ludlow prefers to believe such fortuitous meetings are rooted in the convergence of good ideas. "The what-ifs and good fortune," he reasoned, "can be naturally the result of the right decisions that come together."

Either way, a blossoming business romance was born. In exchange for the Eaton's property, Osmington became a partner in True North, which — with an agreement signed by all three levels of government in 2002 — built a $133-million, 15,015-seat arena on Portage Avenue. "This better work, guys," said the premier. "We've got all our eggs in one basket."

But the Easter Bunny wasn't finished. The relationship between Chipman and Thomson was only just beginning. In fact, Thomson's first visit to the MTS Centre was an Elton John concert (*Benny and the Jets* anyone?) in 2008.

Chipman wasn't looking for a partner to build his arena, yet he ended up in business with the wealthiest man in the country. Not coincidentally, what was once a "quaint thought" of True North acquiring an NHL team quickly morphed into, "This just might work."

KEN GIGLIOTTI WINNIPEG FREE PRES

Eaton's downtown store was an abandoned, decaying hulk by 1999.

David Thomson,
son of David Kenneth
Roy Thomson.

Chipman meets with
Premier Gary Doer and
Mayor Glen Murray to
discuss financing of the
new arena Dec. 19, 2002.

The Timothy Eaton statue surrounded by flowers and cards Oct. 13, 1999.

The store goes down Jan. 7, 2003.

Eaton's famous Grill Room restaurant.

At the April 16, 2003 groundbreaking for the MTS Centre, Premier Gary Doer, Jim Ludlow, president and CEO of True North Sports & Entertainment, and Mark Chipman, chairman of True North, face off at the future site of centre ice.

Chipman as the MTS Centre
rises Sept. 15, 2003.

From Day One, the arena has held more than 150 events per year, consistently ranking in the top-three entertainment venues in Canada, and in the top 20 in North America for non-hockey revenue

After all, the original model of the MTS Centre was sustainable at 120 events (the old arena held around 90 annually), but from Day One, the arena has held more than 150 events a year, consistently ranking in the top three entertainment venues in Canada, and in the top 20 in North America for non-hockey revenue.

Meanwhile, the end of the 2004-05 NHL lockout — which resulted in the establishment of a salary cap tied to revenues — created a seismic shift in the league's financial landscape that also introduced enhanced revenue sharing and guaranteed cost controls.

For the first time in the city's history, the math of NHL hockey began to work. In early 2007, Chipman and Ludlow had their first audience with the NHL's board of governors in New York.

"That was the beginning of the formal process for us where we were asked to present about why Winnipeg would be a viable NHL market," Chipman recalled. "It occurred to me that if they asked us to be there, there was a reason. They were serious about the possibility.

"So from there we just determined... we would just follow it and see where it leads. It was a learning process along the way. There was no particular structure to it. And no matter how much you wanted to advance it, it was something that you didn't have a lot of control over. We took the time to gain as much understanding about as many aspects of the business as we could. Not just the process of getting a team, but how do you operate? What are the real successful models?"

True North was proactive, and Chipman travelled to Edmonton and Ottawa, where both the Senators and Oilers allowed the Winnipeggers to look under their financial hoods. The numbers were encouraging.

As struggling NHL markets began to spew losses and experience various levels of ownership distress, Chipman's phone began to ring. The NHL was calling.

First it was Nashville. Then Phoenix. Then Atlanta.

Through the process, no matter how tempting or how much the NHL might have played hard to get (at least, publicly), True North remained loyal to a singular strategy: patience.

The Northern Lights,
Northern Stars concert
officially opened the
MTS Centre on Nov. 16, 2004.

The Phoenix Coyotes came within a whisker of returning in May of 2010 — within 10 minutes, literally

"We were comfortable in our own skin," Ludlow noted. "We didn't have to make a move. And we weren't about to risk everything we'd built here simply to go to the NHL."

Indeed, if it was a perfect economic storm that led to the loss of the Winnipeg Jets, it was a perfect storm that brought them back — a reverse image of 1995-96.

The Canadian dollar was at par or higher. Six Canada-based teams accounted for more than one-third of all NHL revenue. And more than a few of the NHL's U.S. footprints were being slowly erased by waves of consumer indifference.

"Pieces were in place and the timing was right," Ludlow said. "You can't manufacture that. It has to happen naturally."

Ironically, the same internal and external forces that battered the latter-day Jets — unstable ownership, underwhelming revenue and ever-increasing expenditures — were just as unforgiving on the Coyotes and Thrashers. Phoenix and Atlanta had become the NHL's 21st-century Winnipeg and Quebec City.

"The biggest thing is the confluence of events that found the league struggling in two cities where the franchises weren't coping," noted Don Baizley, the Winnipeg-based agent. "And there's been a number of people for years who said in order for Winnipeg to get back into the NHL there will have to be a few teams in trouble because it's not like we were going to be the first city they'd look at."

In what could only be considered a sea change in decade-long thinking, the NHL's return to Winnipeg became simply a matter of time. In fact, the Phoenix Coyotes came within a whisker of returning in May of 2010 — within 10 minutes, literally — before Glendale's city council agreed to subsidize the team's losses for another season, a figure that was estimated at more than $20 million.

As Glendale councillors dithered, Chipman was in the NHL's head office in New York ready to begin negotiations to buy the destitute club from the league. Meanwhile, Ludlow was back in Winnipeg watching the clock tick down with True North lenders and planning a press conference that had been tentatively scheduled for May 18, 2010 — exactly 15 years to the day of

the Save the Jets rally at Portage and Main — to announce the purchase of the Coyotes.

And that Drive to 13,000 that sold out in less than two minutes almost exactly one year later? True North had that campaign ready to roll in 2010, including ticket prices, sponsorship drives and marketing plans. All of them were in the hopper.

"When you're preparing for D-Day," Ludlow explained, "you're not going to go over the English Channel until you're ready."

Turns out, the extra year before the purchase of the Thrashers only allowed True North to be better prepared. The ticket-price models were refined. The MTS Centre press box was expanded. Blueprints were drawn up to add extra luxury suites. Preliminary discussions for naming rights to the arena (with the addition of an NHL team) were initiated.

If anything, the final acquisition of the Thrashers was decidedly anticlimactic. By early May 2011, reports of the Thrashers' demise had been circulating for weeks. On May 19, the *Globe and Mail*, a newspaper owned by Thomson, reported True North had purchased the Atlanta franchise.

Despite initial denials from both the NHL and True North, all that remained was the waiting. The only thing more inevitable in Winnipeg was winter.

At last, in the wee hours of the morning on May 31, the deal to purchase the Thrashers and relocate the team to Winnipeg was completed after an all-night marathon session of mostly mundane paperwork. When all parties had signed off, there was no backroom celebration.

"I wish I could tell you there were high-fives. There weren't," Chipman said. "It didn't turn out that way."

Instead, Chipman turned out the lights in his office at home and, dead tired, crawled into bed for a few hours of sleep. Ludlow barely slept at all, dropping off at 4 a.m., then being awakened at 5:45 a.m. when a minor legal snag needed to be addressed and put to rest.

Ah, rest. That was a scarce commodity on the eve of the Announcement.

Jim Ludlow, True North Sports &
Entertainment president and CEO,
during the May 31, 2011 announcement
that the NHL would return to Winnipeg.

WAYNE GLOWACKI WINNIPEG FREE PRESS

Mark Chipman (from left), NHL commissioner Gary Bettman, Premier Greg Selinger and David Thomson arrive at the May 31, 2011 news conference to announce the return of the NHL to Winnipeg.

'You're way downstairs. There's no light. Nothing. And we begin to hear all this cheering above us, coming down the stairwell. It sent a chill up my spine'

— Jim Ludlow

At dawn, Chipman drove to the airport to pick up Thomson. They exchanged pleasant greetings and quietly drove to the arena, where furious preparations were being made to stage a press conference to bring the news the entire country knew was coming.

Even the arrival of Chipman's partner didn't go unnoticed, as passengers on the same flight from Toronto were tweeting ahead with breathless word of the 3rd Baron Thomson of Fleet's presence on the plane bound for Winnipeg.

For Chipman, the entire morning was "a bit of a blur." True North officials assembled at the loading dock at the MTS Centre, where NHL brass, led by commissioner Bettman, entered the arena.

After years of persistence, planning and patience, the goal of acquiring an NHL team was suddenly a hazy dream come true.

It was the first time Bettman had set foot in Winnipeg since the ugly unravelling of negotiations to save the Jets in 1995. This visit, no police escort was required.

Instead, the commissioner was given a quick tour of Chipman's humble arena, which met with his approval. "Nice building," he said. "This will do."

Noted Chipman, of Bettman's arrival in the arena's back door: "You try and tell yourself to slow down and take things in, and it's hard. (But) I will always remember that."

As the entourage wound its way around the MTS Centre's lower level, Ludlow kept thinking, "Is this really happening?"

Then came a moment that, for Ludlow, made the happening very real. Remember, the principals at True North had been up all night hammering out the final details of the sale. They didn't have an inkling about what was transpiring outside their bubble.

They were bunkered in the basement of the arena, unaware that word of the impending announcement had spread like viral wildfire — not just throughout the city but the country. Plans had already been announced for an impromptu celebration at The Forks. Police were cordoning off Portage and Main and spontaneous street-hockey games were breaking out amid a mob of a few thousand people who had gathered on an overcast weekday morning.

Unbeknownst to Ludlow, the MTS lobby had also filled with hockey fans spilling in off Portage, transfixed to the in-house television sets waiting for the press conference to begin.

"You're way downstairs," he said. "There's no light. Nothing. And we begin to hear all this cheering above us, coming down the stairwell. It sent a chill up my spine. Those experiences don't come along every day. All of a sudden we realized there's this community all around us that had been waiting for decades for what this group was about to announce.

"It's funny how quickly those kind of moments go by," Ludlow added. "But nobody's going to forget that day."

JOE BRYKSA WINNIPEG FREE PRESS

'Nice building... This will do.'

— Gary Bettman

NHL commissioner
Gary Bettman during
the May 31, 2011
announcement
the NHL would
return to Winnipeg.

Just after 11 a.m., Chipman led a procession to the podium that included commissioner Bettman, longtime friend Ludlow, newfound partner Thomson and Premier Greg Selinger.

As the group took their seats at the table, in a packed room lined at the back with a bank of television cameras, Chipman peeked around the podium to make sure his family members were in the front row, in particular wife Patti. "I wanted to make sure they were there," he said. "She's made a lot of sacrifices over the last 15 years. She really has."

Father Robert was beaming with pride. They're not big about syrupy outbursts of emotion in the Chipman clan. Said Mark: "He is not an 'atta boy' kind of guy. It's more like, 'Keep up the fair work.' "

Then Chipman smiled. "This was never about trying to get my father's approval. That's something we always knew, as kids, that we had."

But there was one face missing — Sheila Chipman, Mark's mother, died in 2005, just three months after the MTS Centre opened. Sheila had been protective of her son during the often-controversial project, which was beset by opponents who wanted to prevent the demolition of the historic Eaton's building.

When the arena opened in November 2004, Sheila Chipman was determined to witness the pomp and ceremony.

"She went through all the agonies of getting the MTS Centre built," Robert Chipman noted. "Those were dark days. She was so excited (when the building officially opened)."

Now in a wheelchair, Sheila also was on hand for a Moose New Year's Eve game to ring in 2005. She died in early February.

"She's the one that would have been tremendously proud," Robert said of the NHL announcement. "Although she would have been a little embarrassed (by the publicity.)"

Had Sheila Chipman been in the front row that day, she would have seen her son step to the podium and say, "I'm excited beyond words to announce our purchase of the Atlanta Thrashers. In a sense, I guess you could say that True North, our city and our province have received a call we've long been waiting for."

Robert Chipman launched the family empire from a used car lot.

Bob and Sheila Chipman

Bettman
congratulates
Chipman.

David Thomson
(from left), Premier
Greg Selinger and
NHL commissioner
Gary Bettman.

Bettman's visit to Winnipeg May 31, 2011, was his first
since April 29, 1995, when he announced the NHL was
leaving. This time, he didn't need police protection.

May 31, 2011 at Portage and Main.

Outside the arena, those words triggered an electrical current of giddy emotion through the streets. Traffic stopped at the famous intersection, just as it did for Hull and Hawerchuk and for the ill-fated rallies to save the Jets years before.

"NHL, welcome home," Premier Selinger added. "We've missed you, and we're going to make it work forever now that you're back.

"Wayne Gretzky once said, 'You shouldn't go where the puck is. You should skate where the puck is going to be,'" the premier added. "And that's what Mark and his team have done. They've skated to where the NHL should be, right back here in Manitoba, right back here in Winnipeg.

"Today we walk with confidence. Today we walk with a feeling that anything's possible."

Offered Thomson: "There's a heartfelt sense of community in Winnipeg, in Manitoba. I've always felt inspired by the leadership and ambitions. And there's been more than a tinge of regret in me — as with all other Winnipeggers and Manitobans — that the Jets left.

"We feel very, very strongly... about the possibilities that lie ahead, to actually move something forward that's distinctive and makes a difference in people's lives. It's about time."

The city was strutting. Yet even as the celebration was about to reach full throat, Chipman was quick to stress that Winnipeg had not just survived the loss of the Jets, but prospered in their absence.

"As important as this may be, I think what is equally if not more important, is the resiliency this community showed over the past 16 years," he said. "And that's why we've gotten another opportunity. We didn't wallow in self-pity."

In many ways, the rise of True North mirrored the economic resurgence of the city, which experienced a construction boom at the turn of this century. Construction cranes were no longer an endangered species. Housing prices spiked to unprecedented levels. Immigration and a stable economy pushed population growth. The city's unemployment rate in 2010 was one of the lowest in Canada.

And development in a two-kilometre radius around Portage and Main — specifically expansions of Red River College, the University of Winnipeg, a $278-million Manitoba Hydro Place

'There's a heartfelt sense of community in Winnipeg, in Manitoba. I've always felt inspired by the leadership and ambitions. And there's been more than a tinge of regret in me — as with all other Winnipeggers and Manitobans — that the Jets left. We feel very, very strongly... about the possibilities that lie ahead; to actually move something forward that's distinctive and makes a difference in people's lives. It's about time.'

— David Thomson

'You look at the city of Winnipeg, it's an act of collective will... Why does a city of this size exist where we are now, miles from any other major city in a community... where it's cold in the wintertime? Why does a city like this exist and continue to develop? It exists because people who live here see the charm of living here: the community. The sense of neighbourliness, the sense of shared commitment to what we're doing'

— Sandy Riley

headquarters, the Canadian Museum for Human Rights (a project estimated at $310 million), the 7,481-seat Shaw Park (home of the Winnipeg Goldeyes independent league baseball team) and The Forks Market — transformed a bulk of the city's downtown core into a vastly more livable environment.

The moral of the story was clear long before Chipman stepped to the podium, according to Sandy Riley, a prominent player in the Save the Jets campaign and CEO of the Richardson Financial Group.

"You look at the city of Winnipeg, it's an act of collective will," Riley said. "Why does a city of this size exist where we are now, miles from any other major city in a community... where it's cold in the wintertime? Why does a city like this exist and continue to develop? It exists because people who live here see the charm of living here: the community. The sense of neighbourliness, the sense of shared commitment to what we're doing. You feel part of something where all the pieces fit together nicely."

Even as Chipman built his arena and patiently laid the foundation for the NHL's return, he offered words of caution: "We have to look at this very soberly," he said in 2007. "We got wrapped up in almost a sense of hysteria about it (in 1995). Unsound, unthoughtful things were being uttered about what was going to happen to the community. There would be a mass exodus. Property values were going to plummet. But more than that, it was

going to be a tremendous blow to our psyche and sense of self-esteem. A death blow, if you believed some people.

"Are we stinging over it still? Absolutely. Is it deep? For sure. Having the NHL in Winnipeg would be a great thing. It's a wonderful asset for a lot of reasons. It could be a signal for young people in the community to give them some hope in where the city is going. And it can make us feel better about where we stand in the North American landscape. We love the game so passionately that it would be great for us to watch it at the highest level.

"But does it define us? Does it make us a great community or not? I don't think it does. We're a great community to begin with."

The absence of the Jets may have made the hearts of Winnipeg hockey fans grow fonder for the NHL. But in the process, perhaps that desire shouldn't be confused with need. Or self-worth.

Former provincial Conservative party leader Stuart Murray is CEO of the Canadian Museum for Human Rights project. But in 2007, Murray was CEO of the St. Boniface Hospital Research Foundation, where his perspective on the loss of the Jets was driven home every day.

"Winnipeg is larger than one sports franchise," Murray reasoned, sipping coffee in the hospital cafeteria. "It just is. I never believed that Winnipeg would dry up and blow away if we lost an NHL team. What we're talking about here is an emotional, intangible element (belonging to the NHL club) that allows you to say we're part of something pretty big and pretty special. But these aren't real-life issues.

"Look, I'll take you up to the palliative care ward here where people are spending their last days on Earth. These people are dying. That's real-life stuff. So would you look at (the loss of the Jets) as a death? That's a little dramatic, perhaps, but it was a loss. With the emotion, someone said it was like ripping the heart out of the community. But maybe we've had a heart transplant. We're still breathing. We're doing well."

Fair enough. But more than a decade after the NHL had departed, Murray still had his last pair of Jets tickets pinned to his bedroom wall. "I'll have them forever," he vowed.

And there's the rub; the small-town Prairie independence colliding with the lingering desire, just beneath the stubble-soiled surface, to feel as worthy as our faraway metropolitan cousins, with their urban roots and big-city sensibilities.

On the day the NHL returned to Winnipeg, a billionaire wearing black sneakers perhaps best summed up those conflicting aspirations.

David Thomson is rail-thin, and he speaks in the low-key cadence of a man reading his own poetry. Thomson's background couldn't be farther from that of his partner Chipman — one man's father started with a dirt parking lot, the other man's father, the 2nd Baron Thomson of Fleet, inherited a media empire and at the time of his death in 2006 had assets estimated at $17.9 billion — but the two men shared a common bond: a passion for hockey and a childhood adoration of Bobby Orr.

Leaning against the wall in a post-press conference interview, Thomson said there was certainly a romantic element involved in ushering the NHL back to a place where hockey is both literally and metaphorically frozen into the cultural fabric.

"Oh, the largest component is definitely passion. No question," he said. "Do I believe there's economics? Absolutely. But it's really to better yourself as a community."

So what of Winnipeg's flourishing development since the NHL left? (Author's aside: Flourishing is a strong word for any description of economic growth involving Winnipeg, but relatively speaking, and based on historical trends, let it stand.)

Thomson paused.

"We all make do, in terms of loss," he said, finally. "But I think you have to understand what's possible when you amplify. When you can have that upper echelon that you aspire to, it's a harder thing to achieve.

"I think it (the NHL's return) fortifies your persona as a city and a province that in my estimation has made some extraordinarily fine moves in the last few years. I believe the NHL offers almost a reaffirmation of principle that comes with many other good things. And we'll find it will be another segue into the psyche of Winnipeggers and Manitobans and one that emits pride and attachment.

"I think it will even draw them closer to a sense of being Canadian," he said. "It's the right to be, in my estimation, a more seminal proposition in terms of touching so many attributes that you'd look for as a citizen. Having something that means something."

It's not as though Winnipeg has never had defining touchstones outside a hockey rink. Wheat and the wheat trade had a symbolism that transcended their reality. So did the railway and the buffalo. So do the Royal Winnipeg Ballet and Monty Hall and Cindy Klassen. So do the Golden Boy and the Guess Who. So may the Jets.

"Things go in cycles," Ludlow said. "Whether it means anything more than it's already meant... I think it's meant we've had some paradigm shifts and defining moments in Winnipeg history that we've experienced in the last couple of years and the last couple of months. You never really understand these things until you live through them and look back (years later). But we're in the midst of the city making history for itself."

No wonder Portage and Main was flooded with joyous hockey fans who, like their city, had been to Hull and back.

After all, there was a little Craig Heisinger in all the fans that day. They never left, either.

And in the end, the NHL came back to them.

'I think it (the NHL's return) fortifies your persona as a city and a province'

— David Thomson

'I think it (the NHL's return) fortifies your persona as a city and a province that in my estimation has made some extraordinarily fine moves in the last few years. I believe the NHL offers almost a reaffirmation of principle that

comes with many other good things. And we'll
find it will be another segue into the psyche
of Winnipeggers and Manitobans and one that
emits pride and attachment'

— David Thomson

Mark Chipman

CHAPTER TEN:

Back in the Bigs

I T'S last call, and Mark Chipman is perched on a bar stool in a steak house in downtown Minneapolis, where he takes a pull on a pint of dark lager.

It's the eve of the 2011 National Hockey League draft, and the next day Winnipeg's newly acquired franchise, just a baby in swaddling clothes, will have the seventh overall selection.

Jets fans at the MTS Centre await Winnipeg's NHL draft pick in St. Paul, Minn., on June 24, 2011.

The mass exultation over the NHL's return had subsided back home, and now the formidable, daybreak-to-dusk task of relocating and overhauling the late Atlanta Thrashers — hiring a front-office staff, evaluating the existing team and preparing the MTS Centre for its new tenant — had begun in earnest.

Chipman had just left another restaurant a few doors down, where the recently crowned Stanley Cup champion Boston Bruins, the cherished franchise of his youth, had burst into the joint as part of a roving celebration tour.

"I met Cam Neely," Chipman reported and sighed just a little. "It's just starting to sink in."

It's understandable. What for so many years had been a conceptual pursuit — when often Chipman had conscientiously preached caution and even open skepticism — was now a reality where the car dealer from Winnipeg was being introduced to one of his hockey idols as an NHL owner.

"It's been a long process," Chipman allowed. "I didn't really know what to expect when it became real. And it didn't seem completely real at first. I was kind of overwhelmed by it. I never really had a chance to take in what was going on in the city and fully grasp the magnitude of it all."

Just days before the deal to purchase the Thrashers was announced, he was asked if he would have difficulty grasping one of life's fortunate mysteries: What happens if your dreams actually come true?

"I know what you're saying," he replied. "Sometimes I'm sitting on my couch watching — flipping back and forth between a couple of games, right? — and for the most part, I do that as anybody else would. And then it occurs to you from time to time that could be us. And it would be very exciting if it were.

"I picture it from time to time, but I don't dwell on it at all," Chipman added. "I think I have a sense of what it's going to feel like. Maybe it's a built-in defence mechanism. I don't want to let people down. I'm not trying to come off all dispassionate and aloof about it. I understand the magnitude of it, I really do. I think about what it's going to look like. I've thought about Ovechkin and Crosby playing in our building, I really have. And that's fun."

But another reality settles in, too, as Chipman mingles with a small group of reporters in the Minneapolis bar, that the unassuming, publicity-shy man who for so long had been "one of us" — who never pretended to be anything more than just another hockey father shuttling his daughters to games or any businessman at chamber of commerce meetings — was now in the company of billionaire NHL owners (some of them, anyway) who from a distance seem inaccessible, whose universe is an unfathomable stratum.

Chipman is the kind of guy who in 2002 jumped in a car and drove to Salt Lake City for the Winter Olympics, then drove right back. He's the kind of guy who shows up to a reporter's engagement party. Even as Chipman nursed his pint, he was fretting about making a flight the next day for home, where he had the all-night chaperone shift at his daughter's high school graduation dance.

This entire NHL business, all of it, was nothing more than a happy accident. His family bought an IHL team because the Jets left, a fateful decision that amounted to little more than community service. The Moose lost a lot of money and weren't even welcomed into a jilted community. The arena concept was the product of the shared vision of two boyhood friends. From the outset, it was never predicated on the NHL's return.

And the part about becoming partners with the richest man in Canada because of an unwanted plot of land? Fairy tales are more believable.

"I wish I could tell you we had this grand plan when I was younger... to own a professional sports team. No, I didn't," Chipman conceded. "I guess the reality of that started 16 years ago. But the fact I've been able to mix my love of hockey and sports and business, and to be surrounded by people of a like mind... if I ever could have scripted something like this when I was younger, it would have looked like this, for sure.

"It's just been a series of good fortune, to be honest with you, and being reasonably prepared to do it at each step. Buying the team, it was new, but I felt good about it. Building the arena, we hadn't done anything like that before, but it felt logical and we had the resources and people to do it. And going down the NHL path,

'... If I ever could have scripted something like this when I was younger, it would have looked like this, for sure'

— Chipman

Chipman watches the Moose practise from high in the stands at the MTS Centre in December 2002.

gradually as we did, we just felt more and more comfortable with it all the way along."

Added Jim Ludlow: "Mark never got out of law school at UND thinking he was going to one day own an NHL team. Not a chance. But the world turns as it does. Planets align for reasons we can't often articulate. And water finds its level."

But isn't Chipman, in many ways, the unlikeliest of NHL owners?

"He doesn't know how likely an owner he is," Ludlow counters. "He's got a very forward-thinking skill set. He's got a passion for hockey. He's a very intuitive, thoughtful guy. Hey, we all did OK in (high) school, but none of us shot the lights out. But Mark has street smarts."

Ludlow described Chipman as having a unique combination of intellect and perspective. He even gave it a name: "intellective."

"If you were able to define the skill sets you would need to become a successful NHL owner, you actually create a Mark Chipman," Ludlow concluded. "Balanced and savvy... like his dad, I guess."

Jim Ludlow, president and CEO of Winnipeg's True North Sports & Entertainment, smiles after announcing all 13,000 Jets season tickets sold in minutes.

MIKE DEAL WINNIPEG FREE PRESS

Chipman would cringe at Ludlow's first string of compliments. He would take considerable pride in the last.

But back to reality, and not the fuzzy, warm early days of bumping into Cam Neely. What of the future? How will all those personal bonds forged in the impressionable years of building the Manitoba Moose withstand the inevitable strain of the NHL? Sure, the Moose never had the comfort of universal acceptance, but they never stirred the dark side of passion, either.

There were no newspaper columns raging for Heisinger's head, even though the Moose never won a championship in their 15 seasons. Fans never flooded the phone lines of radio talk shows to spew venom over a failed draft pick or a disastrous trade.

Question: Will the NHL's arrival threaten the very loyalty and trust the Moose experience created?

Worse, will Chipman and his True North compatriots lose the common-man traits that have so defined their organization, now that they are mingling with NHL elites who for so long considered Winnipeg an afterthought?

"Not at all," Chipman protested. "I think we're very grounded. There's a huge sense of humility in our organization. There had to be. It was imposed on us."

The first test, according to Chipman, was about 15 minutes after season tickets went on sale to the general public and the last one was processed. Suddenly, True North sales representatives became "customer service" representatives. Still, the message was sent out: "Keep it humble. It would be easy to go the other way. But in our hockey department, that will never happen. That's not how these guys are wired."

Heisinger's largest payroll with the Moose was around $3.5 million. In the NHL, that won't get him a second-line centre. So the stakes are much higher, clearly. The microscope is far less forgiving. That doesn't concern Heisinger. "I felt bad when I made a $40,000 mistake," he shrugged. "The $4-million mistake is not going to feel any worse. It's all relative.

"Do I think it's possible that it could change?" Heisinger added. "Yeah, it's possible. But we've built a culture here that we believe in. And I hope we can still do those things and transcend the money and the ego and keep that culture relatively intact. All the little things that were important in the IHL and the AHL days are just as important in the NHL days. It's going to be paramount to keep that in check. And if it starts to slip one day, hopefully somebody points that out to us."

Only time will tell. But according to Ludlow, it's not as though there's even another option to the organization's founding tenets.

"This isn't a transient ownership group that's from Detroit who bought a team in Tampa Bay," the True North CEO reasoned. "We're related to generations of people who are connected to this

Chipman (left)
and Ludlow, in
January 2006.

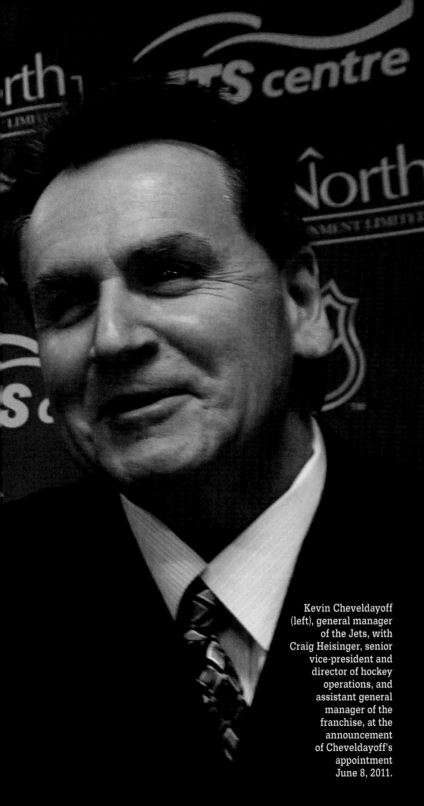

Kevin Cheveldayoff
(left), general manager
of the Jets, with
Craig Heisinger, senior
vice-president and
director of hockey
operations, and
assistant general
manager of the
franchise, at the
announcement
of Cheveldayoff's
appointment
June 8, 2011.

JOE BRYKSA WINNIPEG FREE PRESS

community. It probably would have been cheaper to own a team in another city.

"I don't think this will change our culture, because that will disconnect us from everything that brought us there. I mean, we live in the same place. Our fans live down the street."

Besides, this is the Prairies. Don't believe what people say, believe what they do.

Look no further than Heisinger's first orders of business: the hiring of a general manager and coach for the Winnipeg outfit.

Heisinger could have selected any number of proven, eligible candidates, most notably the GM of the Thrashers, Rick Dudley. Instead, he hired Chicago Blackhawks assistant GM Kevin Cheveldayoff — remember that cocky teenage defenceman with the Brandon Wheat Kings — who for years had served as the Professor Moriarty to Heisinger's Sherlock Holmes (or was that the other way around?) during their heated sparring days in the AHL?

Cheveldayoff's Chicago Wolves were the nemesis of the Moose, and in 12 IHL/AHL seasons, Cheveldayoff teams won four championship titles.

In hiring Cheveldayoff, the personality of Winnipeg's NHL club was already reflecting the lessons and character traits established under Ferguson's Jets and Carlyle's Moose: Reward accomplishment over reputation, give opportunities when they've been hard-earned, and respect rivals who show the qualities you profess to admire.

On the day Cheveldayoff was hired, he was just 41, and like Heisinger, being promoted to an NHL position he'd be holding for the first time.

"It's not going to be easy at times; at times we're going to lean on each other for strength," Cheveldayoff said of Heisinger. "But one thing I can honestly say is I could not have a better man to join me in this building process. Zinger and I go back a long, long way. We met each other when I was a 15-year-old player in Brandon and from that point on, we've had a very, very good friendship, a very, very good rivalry. The relationship that we have is going to be something that is a strength for us in the future."

But perhaps a more telling representation of the DNA of

Claude Noel (left) is introduced as the new head coach of the Jets on June 24, 2011.

Heisinger's team came next. On the morning of the 2011 draft, Cheveldayoff, in concert with Heisinger, hired their first head coach — a 55-year-old hockey lifer, Claude Noel.

You have to understand. Noel was head coach of the Manitoba Moose during their last season, a highly likeable, talkative man who begins almost every morning scrum signalling the level of "joy" in his world. It's usually on the high side.

But the truth is hockey had been a cruel mistress to Noel, who in his two-decade coaching career had been left at the altar too many times to count. In fact, at the end of the 2009-10 season, Noel seemed poised to land his first permanent NHL head-coaching gig after finishing the season as interim head coach of the Columbus Blue Jackets, where he'd served as an assistant for the previous four years.

Noel even led the Blue Jackets, who ultimately missed the playoffs, to a modest 12-10 record down the stretch.

Instead, the Blue Jackets passed Noel over for the young and up-and-coming head coach of the Manitoba Moose, Scott Arniel. Noel was out of work again. But not for long, as Heisinger had long respected Noel's AHL track record, which included a Calder Cup championship with the Milwaukee Admirals in 2004.

Arniel went to Columbus and the NHL. Noel went to Manitoba.

Noel had been jilted enough times to dread getting teased again. In fact, when Chipman was confident that a deal for the Thrashers might happen just after the end of the Moose season in May, he spoke to Noel to make sure his Moose head coach didn't bolt to another organization too soon.

But Noel wasn't excited to hear Chipman's news. On the contrary, he seemed almost cold over the phone. Distant.

Later, Noel explained his reticence to Chipman. "It's Murphy's Law," the son of Kirkland Lake said. "What's always happened in my career is that whatever can go wrong, will go wrong."

That was what Noel was thinking; not that the NHL would come to Winnipeg and finally he would rightly assume the position of head coach. No, Noel was thinking the worst: that the NHL would finally come back to Winnipeg and he would be rejected for the umpteenth time in favour of some more well-known coaching

recyclable. Or a younger, shinier model of himself.

When Cheveldayoff called with the good news, Noel was shopping in the Superstore with Lynda, his wife of 30 years.

"I leaned over a can of tomatoes and it took about a minute before they decided to tell me I had it or not," Noel said. "I would have just rather him say, 'You got the job,' but he didn't, and I went through a living hell for a minute.

"I had daggers flying everywhere. My heart was jumping. There were a lot of emotions. I was really appreciative. Almost tears of appreciation for me. I've gone through this process a few times and I'm a little older (55) and I thought, 'I hope my day is coming.' I thought my day would come."

And it came shopping in a grocery store in Winnipeg. Fair enough. After all, Noel was once fired in a Home Depot when the Nashville Predators cleaned house on the farm in Milwaukee, and Noel left his wife and two sons behind to get a job with the ECHL's Toledo Storm.

Hard roads are not unique in sports. It's just that a lot of them seemed to be leading to Winnipeg. But it all makes perfect sense if you know the franchise heritage. If Noel was good enough to coach the AHL's Moose, he was good enough to coach the NHL team. Why? Because Heisinger thought so, as would Cheveldayoff, who each plowed the exact same field for years.

And it shows, said Chipman.

"That's why I sense from Zing and Chevy there's a real lightness in their step. Claude, too," the owner noted in Minneapolis. "There's this sense of gratification. It just feels better. I wouldn't have wanted to have been dropped into this 15 years ago, or 10 years ago, or even five years ago. I don't think we would have been ready. Now we all talk the same language. There's a comfort and an ease about us. It's not a shiny group. We're going to be what we've been — a hard-working group who won't ever take for granted that we're in this league."

The front office was the first clue of the commitment to the lineage of the franchise. But the exclamation point came in the early evening of the 2011 NHL draft in St. Paul, when Chipman stepped to the podium just prior to his team's selection and, after a

'I'm a little older (55) and I thought, "I hope my day is coming." I thought my day would come'

— Claude Noel

Cheveldayoff welcomes first-round draft pick Mark Scheifele at the 2011 NHL draft in St. Paul, Minn. June 24, 2011.

ERIC MILLER REUTERS

few brief thank-yous, made way for Cheveldayoff and the first pick of the "Winnipeg Jets" — the first use of the franchise's new name. (For added symmetry, the Jets selected a lanky centreman from the OHL's Barrie Colts named Mark Scheifele. His head coach? Dale Hawerchuk.)

Just as the Announcement on May 31, 2011 triggered giddy bedlam in the Winnipeg streets, the official news — in spite of Chipman's understated delivery — launched an instantaneous outpouring of approval. Pockets of Jets diehards in the XCel Energy Center, who had taken the eight-hour trek down Highway I-29 from Winnipeg, were delirious. Back in Winnipeg, more than 4,000 fans who had shown up to watch the draft telecast at the MTS Centre erupted.

True North's choice of name was never a slam dunk. There was a strong sentiment, in fact, for a new name and a fresh start. Remember, the previous NHL Jets never won anything. They lost money. They broke so many hearts. They left.

Still, there was a legacy, a shared source of identity that survived. True North could have named their new team the Polar Bears or the Falcons or the Moose. But how could you bring baseball back to Brooklyn and not call the team the Dodgers? And how would it look when the Winnipeg Polar Bears took the ice for their first game at the MTS Centre, on national television, to the thunderous, relentless chants of "Go Jets Go!"

In the end, it was really no choice at all.

"It isn't about me," Chipman said. "I'm not trying to sound altruistic here, but when they say you own the team... well, you do and you don't. It's not right just to impose my will on this. It (the Jets name) has almost taken on mythical proportions.

"Besides, that's how I got in — to save the Winnipeg Jets. I thought long and hard about how much it meant back then and how much it means to the community. It was the right thing to do."

But if you think a large constituency of Manitoba hockey fans was adamant that the new NHL team be called the Jets, they couldn't hold a candle to a player like Thomas Steen, who for so long held a torch for the only NHL team he'd ever known.

Fans at the MTS Centre go wild when it's announced at the NHL draft in St. Paul, Minn., on June 24, 2011, that Winnipeg's new team would be called the Jets.

'And when they named them the Jets my tears came. I wasn't even crying, but the tears just came. I couldn't stop it. It was just pure joy. Unbelievable'

— Thomas Steen

Just last October, the longest-serving Jet in franchise history was elected to Winnipeg city council. It was the first time Steen had found full-time employment in Winnipeg since his bittersweet retirement at The Funeral ceremony in 1995.

In the years that followed, Steen, whose son Alex is currently toiling for the St. Louis Blues, would serve as a scout for a handful of NHL teams, always living out of a suitcase.

"I felt rootless," Steen said, sitting at a conference-room table at Winnipeg's city hall. "Especially being a scout (for other teams) and flying around on the road three weeks a month all year. You come back and sleep for two or three days and then you're on the road again. I did that for years. It was a weird feeling.

"Now I know how bad I felt over the years about that," the old centreman-turned-civic politician added. "When I would go around scouting, you'd see a retired player come out to give out an award or being honoured by the team. Or they're at the game hanging out. In St. Louis, they have a suite for the older players. But my team was gone. I couldn't go back and enjoy it. I got jealous. I remember seeing Ken Morrow come out on the ice on Long Island and thinking, 'God, I wish I could do that.' Just to be part of it in some way."

How deeply is Thomas Steen connected to the Jets' name? On the afternoon of the draft in St. Paul, where Chipman was going to make the announcement official that night, word was spreading around city hall that it would be the Jets. Steen was sitting with a couple of his aides, having coffee, when a second reliable source confirmed the impending news.

Tears started streaming down Steen's cheeks.

"I never thought it was going to happen either, that the team would come back," he said. "And when they named them the Jets my tears came. I wasn't even crying, but the tears just came. I couldn't stop it. It was just pure joy. Unbelievable."

But why was the name so important?

"I don't know," Steen said. "All the sweat and injuries. All the guys I played with. I got a bunch of emails from older players telling me I had to get out there and fight for the Jets name."

After all, Steen arrived in Winnipeg as a Swedish immigrant, a young man barely in his 20s, who after 14 seasons in a Jets uniform found a home.

"I fought so hard to play my whole career here," he said. "I knew I could get traded any day. They'd pack my bags (a teammate's prank) once in a while to scare me. I worked like a dog to stay. We had it so good. I feel like I know everyone in town. Everywhere you go, there's friends."

Of course, Steen isn't the only former player with a special place reserved in his heart for the Jets. Sure, that franchise left for Phoenix long ago. The Coyotes have all the Jets records and have even inducted former Jets Bobby Hull, Steen and Dale Hawerchuk into the team's ring of honour.

But that must have seemed a hollow ritual for the Jets players and the Phoenix fans alike. Traditions and memories can't be carted from city to city in moving vans.

"When you look at the league and all of these teams, you picture Bobby Clarke in a Flyers jersey," Hawerchuk noted. "You picture Jean Beliveau in a Montreal jersey, you can picture Darryl Sittler in a Toronto jersey."

And you picture Dale Hawerchuk in a Jets jersey.

"When I went to Winnipeg, Bobby Hull was one of my idols," Hawerchuk explained. "I remember him skating around in that Jets jersey, and I enjoyed skating in the same jersey that he did. It made me proud to be a Winnipeg Jet. History is a big part of it.

"I think you can say that for all the guys that played there. When the Jets were coming back, all the guys (former players) started emailing each other. For sure, you'd love to see the team again and watch the team and cheer for a team you used to be a huge part of. It's great they're back."

Such sentiments are not confined to Hawerchuk's era, either.

"Whether I was an NHL Jet or a WHA Jet, it doesn't matter," offered Joe Daley, the longest-serving member of the original Jets. "I was part of professional hockey in Winnipeg. To me, if I can do anything for them... I know any of the guys locally would be honoured to represent what we thought Winnipeg meant to us. Especially a guy like me who came home to play and never regretted it. I look back on it as the best decision I ever made."

And what message would Daley pass on to the Jets of the 21st century? "You'll love to play here," he replied. "You'll be kings in this town. They'll embrace you. They'll make you feel like you're the best person in the world. That's what guys like us can pass on to anybody."

There's a very rural, distinctly small-town metaphor for the loss of the Winnipeg Jets, instantly recognizable to anyone who grew up in a tiny community only to see it wither and disappear. The school closes. The grain elevator is torn down. The senior hockey team that carried the town's name and colours folds.

For Steen, the Winnipeg Jets became his ghost town. There was no going home anymore. No hometown reunions to see old faces and tell old stories. And it wasn't just Steen who felt rootless.

"Let's be honest, everybody, especially old athletes, wants to belong to something," said former Jets forward Jordy Douglas, who is currently the president of the club's shrinking alumni association. "We all have a history. It's always kind of cool to be remembered. Now that the NHL is back in town... you have to believe with everything the new franchise has done, they understand the history of the game and the connection to the old guard. Mark Chipman and Craig Heisinger, they know the history of the game in Manitoba.

"So will this be a home for the old guard? I really believe that to be true."

Yes, there are deep roots. There's baggage. There are generations of shared memories and disappointments and triumphs that wouldn't have meant a damn thing if the fan in the next seat or the neighbour in next house weren't wearing white, too.

Was that collective identity lost when the Jets died in 1996? Or was it only found because they left in the first place?

How do you live up to the romanticized version of the Jets past — given an understanding of the star-crossed histories of the deceased franchises that came before — and move forward into the future?

No wonder Chipman, in moments of sober clarity, can already feel the burden of redefining his city's history.

How do you live up to the romanticized version of the Jets past — and move forward into the future?

> ‘I don't think people just want an NHL franchise... they want a successful one. You have to win. You want something that people are really proud of'
>
> —Mark Chipman

"I'm not an unemotional guy," he said. "In fact, I've been accused of being the exact opposite. But there's a lot at stake here, so I try to separate the emotion out of it. It's more of a head-down approach. What I think about more is what it's going to take to be successful at it. So you have a big opening night and everybody's fired up. But this is our home and we have to be successful at this. It's daunting. It's a very, very competitive league.

"So what I spend more time thinking about is how are we going to differentiate ourselves? How are we going to be successful? What are we going to do that will make it an asset that everybody wants it to be?

"I don't think people just want an NHL franchise," Robert Chipman's son concluded, "they want a successful one. You have to win. You want something that people are really proud of."

What the future holds, however, is but a continuation of a journey that began, once upon a time, with a motley collection of outcasts and outlaws boarding Northwest Orient Flight 215 to New York City and the unknown. They had names like McDonald, Daley, Hull and Cadle. And who could have predicted what would befall their Jets descendants, or the city whose fans would one day wear white at their funeral?

Yes, it's been a long, crazy journey from the day Benny Hatskin asked, "How would you like to see Bobby Hull in Winnipeg?" to Mark Chipman's first inkling that, "This just might work."

Whether it was fate that Lazer Hatskin missed the maiden voyage of the Titanic by six days or that Dr. Gerry Wilson was given a Swedish intern named Anders Hedberg, is a matter of wistful debate. Just like the odds of Chipman's accidental partnership with a billionaire baron.

After all, sometimes the future just unfolds, and history is the only judge of cosmic coincidence.

On April 28, 1972, when Bobby Hull was still a twinkle in Benny Hatskin's eye, a column appeared in the *Winnipeg Free Press*, buried in the back section of the sports pages. It was written by the late Reyn Davis, who would document the travails of the Jets for the next two decades. He was clearly miffed that the NHL had recently granted a franchise to the city of Atlanta, located in America's Deep

JOE BRYKSA WINNIPEG FREE PRESS

Chipman smiles during the May 31, 2011 announcement of the NHL's return to Winnipeg.

'OUR best days in the game are ahead of us... not behind... It's taken imagination, guts and bags of money, plus the resolve in the face of widespread cynicism, to go into the same business as the National Hockey League.

This is one resource that isn't going to slip away. And for once, it's up to us'

— Reyn Davis, sports columnist, Winnipeg Free Press

South, while snubbed fans in the game's heartland were forced to seek refuge in the fledgling WHA.

"Is there anything about Winnipeg that is so second-class, people must leave the city to be successful?" Davis wrote. "Isn't it just about time this city put its priorities in order? It galls me to think we should be so gullible as to breed and hatch hockey players like cooped-up hens in some artificially lit hatchery for the savoury delights of the rednecks in Atlanta, Ga. If Winnipeg isn't more entitled to a National Hockey League franchise than Atlanta, then (NHL president) Clarence Campbell really must wear star-spangled pyjamas to bed at night.

"If Winnipeg can pay them as much, treat them just as kind and be first-class in every respect, can there be anything wrong with a player spending his best years here and not Atlanta?

"Our best days in the game are ahead of us... not behind," Davis concluded. "It's taken imagination, guts and bags of money, plus the resolve in the face of widespread cynicism, to go into the same business as the National Hockey League. This is one resource that isn't going to slip away. And for once, it's up to us."

Nothing's changed, of course. Those words ring as true today as they did when a team called the Winnipeg Jets represented little more than a city's modest hope for a better future.

Granted, it was just a hockey team, but maybe it would come to mean much more. Put the place on the map. Perhaps it would help a small Canadian city let the world know it was still there, thriving. Vibrant enough to compete at the highest level in a nation where the game mattered.

And now? If the past has taught anything, the answer to that question is simple: Who knows? Was there a baby born in Helsinki today, or Winnipeg, or even Shanghai, who could 30 years from now have Jets fans chanting his name? Will the Jets play in Stockholm again one day, only this time with the Swedish team being an NHL rival?

The possibilities are endless. The future has yet to be written. And like all Jets stories, it ends at the beginning.

Portage and Main awaits.